# FIRE ON THE EARTH

STEPHEN J. ROSSETTI

ON THE
EARTH

Daily Living in the
Kingdom of God

TWENTY-THIRD PUBLICATIONS
**Mystic, Connecticut**

This work is dedicated to

THE QUEEN OF PEACE

Twenty-Third Publications
P.O. Box 180
185 Willow Street
Mystic, CT 06355
(203) 536-2611

ISBN 0-89622-391-4
Library of Congress Catalog Card Number 88-51808

# Foreword

For over two decades my brother, as Entertainment Editor of the *Los Angeles Times*, has been reviewing movies. From the outset his policy was to judge films not by the personal lives of the actors, but by the quality of their professional performances.

In some ways, we should follow the same approach with a book, judging the volume by its content, not by the author's personal life. Nevertheless, with books on spirituality and prayer, there may be justification for delving into the writer's background.

One reason, of course, is that personal knowledge of the author increases interest in reading the book and supplies added motivation to grasp the ideas presented. More significant, however, is the often personal nature of a publication on the spiritual life. When a book reflects the writer's own experiences and seeks to influence the reader's way of living, then some knowledge of the author becomes helpful and even critical, if the publication is to exert maximum impact.

Father Stephen Rossetti's book is personal in both respects. First of all, in this volume he reflects on his own experiences. He discloses a bit of himself within its pages, he occasionally reveals something about his family, he frequently cites examples from his ministry, and he clearly has drawn the book's insights from extended moments of reflective, private prayer.

Second, he seeks to influence the reader's way of living. I have read his manuscript twice, once in its primitive draft and then in the finished version. During both perusals, the book caused me to squirm uneasily in my chair. Fire, after all, gives warmth and light, but it also blisters and burns, consumes and destroys, even as it purifies.

These brief, incisive, and challenging chapters forced me to examine my own lifestyle and that evaluation made me uncomfortable at times. As Father Rossetti observes, one must acknowledge the darkness, the wounds, and the weakness before God's light, healing, and strength can enter us.

Who, then, is this Stephen Rossetti who writes personally and tries to influence our personal lives? His path to the priesthood was not an "out of high school, years in the seminary, and on to the altar" kind of journey. After a public school education and graduation from the Air Force Academy, he served his required tour of duty as an officer in the Air Force and during this period mastered, among other things, the technique of parachute drops.

Some type of an inner conversion led him then to consider a vocation to the religious life. Steve first entered a strict monastic contemplative community before eventually deciding to seek admission into the diocesan priesthood.

While pursuing theological studies at the Catholic University of America, his insights about the interior life and his skills as a writer surfaced, at that early stage, in the form of articles and reviews for journals on spirituality.

He became Father Rossetti at age 33 and has served as an associate pastor for six years in two busy urban parishes. In addition to the standard parochial duties, he provided regular spiritual guidance for a considerable number of directees and conducts ongoing sessions on prayer. Somehow, in the midst of all this, the thin bespectacled priest has been able to write two books, the present volume and an earlier work, *I Am Awake: Discovering Prayer* (Paulist Press). As one who has produced a few texts over the years while engaged in full-time parish ministry, I know that he could accomplish so much only with great self-discipline, sustained hard work, and a draining expenditure of energy.

Steve, at the same time, plays a superior game of squash and golf, frequently enjoys a good movie, and meets regularly with close friends. Committed to a radically simple, but still joyous and healthy lifestyle, Rossetti practices what he preaches: finding Jesus Christ at the center of his life through daily periods of prolonged prayer.

His first book grew out of the experiences of teaching people how to pray, although it naturally flowed as well from his own personal and serious dedication to the spiritual life. *Fire on the Earth*, on the other hand, emerges essentially out of his prayerful reflections on Scripture, although it simultaneously draws deeply upon his rich pastoral encounters.

This is not a book to be read through at one sitting. Instead, it deserves and needs to be taken a bite at a time, like one chapter or section each day with space and moments for prayerful reflection after every reading.

Father Stephen Rossetti's latest contribution will quite likely stir a fire in the reader's mind and heart where, after all, God's kingdom can be found.

*Rev. Msgr. Joseph M. Champlin*

## Acknowledgments

A word of thanks to Mary Ellen Vasile who read parts of the manuscript and offered helpful comments. A special thanks to Gregg Ginn, Fr. Joseph Champlin, Helene Rossetti, John and Kathy Colligan, and all the people of St. James Parish. Each played an important role in the development of this work and, more importantly, in encouraging and challenging me as a person, as a Christian, and as a writer. From the bottom of my heart, I say to you all, "Thank you."

## Author's Note

Inclusive language was used whenever possible. Biblical citations were taken from the New American Bible since this translation is used in the current lectionary. Where inclusive language is inserted, it is noted by brackets. The phrase "Kingdom of God" is used instead of the "Reign of God" because of the former's concrete and spatial connotations. Such connotations are critical to this work.

Likewise, the male gender is used occasionally when referring to God in deference to Scripture, tradition, and for ease of writing. While it may strike some as an example of sexism, I do not mean it to be so. It should be noted that God is neither male nor female but transcends both and is the source of both. I ask the patience of all readers with this sensitive and important issue.

# Contents

# Introduction

I often ask the following question: "If you were to summarize the message of Jesus of Nazareth in one line, what would it be?" To phrase it another way, "If you were with Jesus during his ministry, what theme would be reiterated again and again so as to form the core message of his proclamation?"

The gospels of Matthew (4:17), Mark (1:15), and Luke (4:43) all clearly summarize his message with the same basic line. Direct references to this reality occur at least forty-eight times in Matthew, sixteen times in Mark, and thirty-seven times in Luke.[1] It is clear and precise. Do you know what it is?

I never get the right answer. Ministers, priests, sisters, and lay people alike usually respond with such phrases as, "God is love." Or they will say, "Do unto others as you would have them do to you." Some add, "Love God and love neighbor." These are indeed important parts of the gospel message and are authentic teachings of Jesus. However, they are not the core proclamation of his preaching.

The core message goes beyond these phrases. While these and others are an essential part of Christianity, they do not capture the essence of the gospel message. Such teachings are all found in a number of other religions around the world, yet there is something unique about our religion that makes it completely unlike any other. There is something about our faith that transcends even the most exalted of other spiritual teachings in the world.

The core message is this: *The kingdom of God is at hand.* Christianity is not based on an idea or a new teaching or a new moral code, though it does include such things. Rather, it is based upon an historical event. Something happened at a particular point in history that never happened before and will never happen again. It is an act so dramatic as to change the entire course of history and each of us besides. This act is the breaking into our human history of the Kingdom of God. The phrase "the Kingdom of God" refers to the power, presence, or rule of God, or indeed, God's very self. When Jesus says this presence or rule is "at hand," he means that it is here right now. "At hand" conveys a current event, that it is right now in the act of touching the created world.

How did this happen? Consider Marshall McLuhan's insight, "The medium is the message." Jesus proclaimed the Kingdom and thus he was the medium. But he was also the message. It is in Jesus himself that God has come into the world. He is not only fully human, but also fully divine. It is in this God-man that the Kingdom of God has come.

You might object, "Yes, but there are other religions in which gods become human." However, this is not true. Their gods may take on the mask of being human; they may spend time meddling in human affairs, often to the chagrin of mortals, but they do not really become human. They are not born. They do not have a human heart, a human mind, a human will. They do not suffer and cry. They do not thirst and bleed. And, most of all, their gods cannot die.

This concept of God becoming human and breaking into our history is, as the sons of Abraham cried out, blasphemous. It blasphemes the very transcendence of the infinite God. It is impossible by any calculation of the human mind and thus is incomprehensible to our limited intellects. It is a message that is so radical as to rock every basic religious principle before this event.

The Kingdom of God is at hand! God's very self is coming into our world. He does not wear a human mask, nor is this presence simply the immanence of God, who dwells in every heart and every molecule of his creation. It is more. The Creator becomes part of creation, and walks the face of the earth.

No wonder they killed Jesus. They had to. Such an event demands a total self-surrender or a total rejection; there can be no middle ground. The message is too strong; it demands a radical response. If they did surrender themselves to it, it would have required a painful transformation: a letting go of everything they had known and a launching into a vague and uncertain future. Few were willing to do so.

In these pages, we will step into this outrageous phenomenon and open ourselves to the power and the promise of this event. May we truly experience the core message of Jesus: The Kingdom of God is at hand. By doing so, we will rediscover what it means to be a Christian. We will have rediscovered *basic Christianity*.

# WHERE IS
# THE KINGDOM?

# 1

# Are You Born Again?

🐦     I was sitting quietly on an airplane, expecting an uneventful ride, when the middle-aged woman next to me asked, "Have you been saved?" Taken aback, I stammered some response that only indicated to her that my eternal prospects were perilous, but not completely without hope. She then launched on an evangelical, fundamentalist proclamation of the gospel and for the rest of the flight I was a captive audience.

As this woman talked, she spoke of her own salvation in Christ and referred to a specific date. She said, "I was saved five years ago, on March 20, in the morning during a prayer service." To lifelong members of traditional Christian churches, this approach is hard to understand.

We believe that we are incorporated into the saving mystery of Christ through baptism, a notion well-founded in the Scriptures. As it says in the gospel of Mark, "The [one] who believes in it [the Good News] and accepts baptism will be saved" (16:16). With flowing water and invoking the Trinity, the person is brought into the economy of salvation and the rest of his or her life is a deepening of this life in Christ begun in baptism.

And yet so many do not feel saved. Those baptized as infants especially do not consciously "experience" this salvation. They have a certificate of baptism in their hands, but it is only a piece of paper. Many, usually only semiconsciously, search for a personal awareness of this salvation. They wish to know this redemption for themselves; it is the human quest. It is no wonder, then, that many evangelical, fundamentalist churches are thriving today. They provide a favorable setting for just such an experience and a theology that supports it.

When the woman next to me said she was saved, naming the specific date, she was referring to just such an experience. God touched her life that day in a powerful way. She knew for the first time by experience that God had a personal love for her and nothing could separate her from this love, not "trial, or distress, or persecution, or hunger, or nakedness, or danger, or the sword" (Rm 8:35). Armed with this experiential knowledge of God's redemptive love and cognizant that nothing could stop it, she displayed a true Christian confidence that she expressed by the phrase, "I have been saved." She was then baptized into her church.

In the early apostolic church, such occurrences were common. Cornelius, for example, first received the Holy Spirit and only after this experience was baptized (Acts 10:47). For others, the experience of salvation came only upon or after baptism. The scales fell from Saul's eyes only after Ananias laid hands on him and then baptized him (Acts 9:17-18). Whether the Holy Spirit comes before or after baptism, there is an implication that the reception of both are related.

Because of such gospel accounts, and because of her own experience, the woman did not believe that one is saved without this spiritual experience. The problem with such an approach is obvious: What about those who are baptized but have not "experienced" the Kingdom of God? Are they not saved?

The plight of these people is poignantly described by a woman in a prayer group who wrote:

> I know many people who have been touched by the Kingdom—an experience of God. But I have "asked," "knocked," "sought," given up and waited. Nothing works. It is like continually being told I have a Father who loves me, yet never being picked up in His arms and hugged. What good are words and knowledge if that experience is missing? And how can you possibly bring others into a relationship you have not experienced yourself? If God wants workers in His vineyard, why doesn't He accept those who apply and tell them what to do? Whenever I think of this I am embarrassed and cry. I feel so much pain.

Our hearts go out to this persevering woman and it is hard to fathom why God does not answer her prayer. I suspect that my airplane companion would tell her that although she was not yet saved she should keep praying—one of these days God will save her.

This explanation is difficult to accept. Something in our hearts tells us that a person who prays daily for the grace of salvation, longs for it with all her being, is already inside the saving body of Christ. Do not the Scriptures speak of a God that continually offers the grace of salvation to all people and rejoices in the one lost sheep? Rather than keeping people out of the heavenly banquet, he drags them in from the highways and hedgerows to fill up his house (Lk 14:23).

Perhaps there is a fundamental flaw in equating salvation with a profound experience of God's love. While the latter is a consoling spur to faith and a possible sign of election, salvation is a much broader reality and encompasses a larger multitude. In fact, it is such a complex and profound mystery that no one church or denomination can adequately express it alone. It takes many understandings of faith to make up the larger body of Christ.

Still, as a foundation, we might begin with the proclamation ascribed to Peter in Acts: "There is no salvation in anyone else, for there is no other name in the whole world given to [us] by which we are to be saved" (4:12). Time and again Paul will tell us that we are saved by faith in this name. More than just a notional assent to a statement about the identity of Jesus, faith is a deeply personal response to this person. To "believe" is to look upon God as Father and to call his son savior and Lord. We look to him as a good shepherd who is leading us safely home.

My father would never call himself a mystic nor claim to have had a dramatic experience of the divine. But when he speaks of Jesus, there is a warm tone in his voice when he calls him "the Good Lord." It communicates humility, respect, and a feeling of hope. Such are the marks of faith; they are signs of salvation.

We all rejoice with the "saved" woman who, by an extraordinary grace of God, experienced a brilliant flash of the Kingdom of God. Incidentally, at the end of a very long plane ride, after I had heard everything she said, I responded to the Good News of salvation as I truly felt. I said, "I believe." She then quoted the gospel of Mark and said, "You are not far from the reign of God" (12:34). We parted, both of us feeling much better. I had redeemed myself and she had another soul for Christ.

To the second woman, still without such a glorious experience, we might ask, "Is God not in the darkness as well?" Is the saving mystery of Christ any less present on Calvary than it is on Mount Tabor? Sometimes we are called to rest in his glory; other times we are to descend into our darkness and pain and seek him there.

And all those who are saved share a common hope, a similar vision: We look to Jesus. We call his Father our Father; we call him savior and Lord. And, like Peter who was frightened and began to sink in the water, we look to him and cry out, "Lord, save me" (Mt 14:30).

# 2

# God Makes All Things Good

    Little Meredith, five and one-half years old, was run over by a car in her own driveway. Sadly, her own parents, John and Betsy, were behind the wheel. There was no fault, no excessive speed, no carelessness, just the enthusiasm of a child who was playing and not looking where she was going.

For the past six weeks, Meredith has been fighting for her life while her parents keep vigil by her bedside. Her brothers and sisters are struggling to understand the meaning of the tragedy, apparently without much success.

At different moments, each sibling walked into the parents' bedroom and asked the difficult questions, "Why did this happen? Why would God do such a thing?"

The standard theological answer is that God did not "do" it. Our creator made a world without evil and pain, which is symbolized in Genesis by the Garden of Eden. However, since we were given the gift of free will, some choices made by humans were against goodness, against God, against love. Thus sin, pain, and suffering entered the world. In the language of Genesis, Adam and Eve were expelled from the Garden to labor and toil.

Unfortunately, such an answer would not make much sense to a young child, or an adult for that matter, who is struggling with the existence of innocent suffering in the world. It is not fair; no amount of theological justification can make it so. The heart cries out in shock and disbelief. How could such a thing happen? Who would allow such an enormous evil?

John and Betsy knew instinctively that their children were not looking for a theological response. They said simply, "It was an accident. We are all upset and sad for Meredith. Tragedy has struck others; it can happen to us." Like their children, John and Betsy feel the pain. They themselves do not understand the mystery of such "senseless" evil; yet something else was communicated to their children, not so much by what they said as how they said it.

There is peace in their hearts, an acceptance of the tragedy, as difficult as it is. Though they do not understand, they are able to live with this "not understanding." Somehow in the core of their hearts they are able to reconcile the existence of such evil with the rule of a good and compassionate God. Their children must have subconsciously felt their parents' acceptance and peace, and moved deeper into this mystery of life.

So many adults are not able to reconcile this "contradiction." They cannot accept the goodness of life, their own goodness, and the rule of a good God with the presence of evil and suffering. This internal contradiction becomes a chasm in people, which eventually widens and rips them apart.

Two men came to me separately within a one week period; both had lost their wives about ten years ago. One had turned to drink and self-pity. Because of the trauma, he had lost his faith and was crumbling—physically, emotionally, and spiritually. It was hard to witness. The other had no formal religion previous to the disaster. "But," he said, "when she died, something seemed to call me. I felt that my life was missing an important piece and I realized that it had something to do with God." He converted to Christianity and now is a productive and happy lay minister in our church. I left his presence with a feeling of joy and thanksgiving.

There are many reasons why people stop practicing their faith. Oftentimes it is a result of conflict, perhaps a conflict with a person such as a minister. It can be a moral conflict: They fall into an immoral practice and rather than give it up, they give up their religion. But many leave because of this internal conflict—a good God allows senseless pain and suffering.

The first step in finding a reconciliation of this conflict is *to accept our own pain and suffering.* In spiritual counseling, people often become "stuck" and make no progress, as if there is a wall through which the person refuses to pass. Many times the wall is a shield that blocks an enormous pain.

To allow the person to begin to live and to move along the path of healing and wholeness, the counselor gently explores the nature of the block and helps the person to move beyond it. What follows often are waves of pain and tears as a powerful hurt is brought to the surface and slowly healed. When people begin to feel and accept their own personal pain, they have taken a large step in coming to grips with the reality of human suffering. How many people reject God and religion because of the existence of pain, yet while they are speaking of it, their faces are contorted with their own unrecognized and unhealed pain!

As Meredith was healing, I spoke with her mother at length. At one point she said something that stopped me cold. "I feel badly for those people who don't have such a tragedy, people who go through their entire lives without any crisis or disaster." When I asked why, she responded, "Because of this, I see the trees differently, the flowers, peoples' faces. I feel like I see so much more." When I asked if she thought this new perception would wear off, she said, "No. I'm different because of the experience. From the very beginning I have felt God's presence and I know that a blessing has come with this tragedy."

When people say such things, these are sometimes merely the pious platitudes of people who have not dealt with the pain and suffering. This is not true of Betsy. Her comment came from the heart; I knew it was true. It is so similar to the thought of St. Therese of Lisieux: "Suffering is, of all the things God can give us, the best gift. He gives it only to his chosen friends."[1] Such an insight reveals a level of consciousness well beyond the mere acceptance of pain.

Arriving at this insight usually requires much human struggle and toil, but in the end it is clearly a gift. Perhaps it comes when the heart, battered by the reality of its own suffering and unanswered questions, looks to a higher power for help. Julian of Norwich, the fourteenth-century English mystic, arrived at just such a condition. When she prayed for help she received this answer, "All shall be well, and all shall be well, and all manner of thing shall be well."

This is not to say that human suffering will not continue. Living during the end of the Middle Ages, Julian experienced a world of "violence, cruelty and pessimism."[2] Nor is it a belief in a future universal salvation. In one of her mystic revelations, she saw the devil and his creatures that were cast out by the power of God. Rather, it is a deep, intuitive sense—one that Betsy has, one that St. Therese shares also. It is hard to express because the grace is beyond the capacity of words. St. Paul tried to express a similar sentiment when he said that "God makes all things work together for the good of those who love him" (Rm 8:28). Suffering and pain become rich moments of grace when experienced by a heart transformed by faith. Even Satan's actions are mysteriously taken up into the divine will to bring forth the Kingdom of God, much to his rage.

Christians are not exempt from human suffering. In fact, there is a vital connection between it and transformation. The Christian experience is as much found on Mount Tabor in transfiguration as it is on Calvary in crucifixion. But there is a special conviction that sets apart the Christian heart. Deep within there is a sense that no evil, no matter how seemingly senseless and unjust, is in vain. Rather, in the mystery of divine providence, it is taken up and transformed. The darkness becomes a brilliant light.

Such a conviction is truly a grace. It comes to the heart that opens itself beyond what can be seen and felt. It may come in a flash as it did for Julian of Norwich or it may come through a personal tragedy as it did for Betsy. But when it does come, the human heart rests in an indescribable peace because it knows that "all shall be well, and all shall be well and all manner of thing shall be well."

# 3

# How Do We React to Pain?

🕿 A couple of days ago, an attractive young woman approached me. I noticed her face had in it some unexpected lines of anguish. The reason for their existence became clear during the course of her story. She was an alcoholic and life had been hard. Alcoholics Anonymous had helped her find sobriety but she confessed that she needed something more. "I've started sitting in the church and praying," she said. "How has it been going?" I asked. "Pretty good; I'm starting to feel good about myself. I feel like reaching out to help others." She added, "I think I know why I drink. I have been unhappy; I drink not to feel the pain."

We are all unhappy. In the very core of our hearts is a restlessness, a lack, an incompleteness. It is hard to face this fundamental pain. We believe there is something wrong with us for having this pain. Some deny it, cover it up, drown it in drink.

Human beings are very creative in the many ways they deny this pain. While this woman turned to drink, others use different forms of sensual gratification: food, sex, drugs, excessive activity and entertainment. Or we slowly anesthetize ourselves in front of the television. While all these sensual pleasures can be good, their abuse is deadening. They put us to sleep.

Other ways of covering up the pain are more subtle. We can lose ourselves in work, in striving for achievement, power, or prestige. We can cling to our spouses, our children, ourselves, or even our "religion" as a narcotic to relieve the pain. The spouse who expects perfection from the other, the parents who drive their children unmercifully, the priest who spends all of his time giving to others without personal prayer, all refuse to face the pain in their own hearts.

To find an answer, we first must accept the question. To be healed, we first feel the hurt. Indeed, there is a question; there is a hurt. Something is lacking in us and we will never be happy until we understand what it is we truly lack and come to find it for ourselves.

I was in a monastery on retreat for a month. It was initially a difficult experience. The transition from an active ministry to the exterior and interior silence of the monastery is a hard one. The building was cold; the food was limited; and there were few distractions.

To those who accuse monks of running from reality, I can only say that they have never experienced such silence. It is a hothouse for humanity. The force of one's humanity comes to the forefront in a rage. I would have given much for a two-hour escape into the dream world of a movie.

When my retreat ended, I took a bus home from the monastery. On the bus a surprising realization came over me. Something was very wrong; the people seemed very unhappy. At first, I thought some tragedy must have befallen them to cause such sadness. Moments later I realized that nothing had happened—they were always like this!

Why have I only now noticed the world's sadness? "Ah!" I thought, "I have just come from the monastery." As hard as life was there, a sense of joy and peace permeated the community. It was so subtle and taken for granted that no one noticed it, except an occasional visitor. I, too, had taken it for granted. But now, with the consciousness of the Kingdom of God, I recognized its striking absence on that bus.

No one was more aware of the pain and weariness of our world than the Son of Man. He called out to us in our need: "Come to me, all you who are weary and find life burdensome, and I will refresh you. Take my yoke upon your shoulders and learn from me, for I am gentle and humble of heart. Your souls will find rest" (Mt 11:28-30).

Frankly, we do not believe his words. Our intellects nod and say "yes" but there is a corner of our hearts that says, "No, stay away from me." We are wary and fearful of God and his voice echoing in his Son. Food, drink, sex, and many other diversions seem more sure to us; they promise a quick and safe moment of rest—an escape. But the voice of God is hard to hear especially when it asks us to let go of what we can see in order to trust in something we cannot.

Have you ever accompanied an alcoholic through the stages of recovery? It is a horrible and gut-wrenching process. No other difficulty causes such internal agony and requires such superhuman courage and strength.... But the plain fact of the matter is that we are all addicts. We are addicted to the safe pleasures of the world and refuse to let go of them to touch God. As long as we are unable to let go, though, we will be like the people on the bus: unhappy and not even aware of our misery.

I remember the first time another woman came in for spiritual direction. My initial impression was of an enormous sadness. Her face had the pallor of death. The strange part was that she acted as if everything were fine. The world concurred. Joyce was a successful community leader whose prosperous life was spent working and achieving.

During the first session, she was stunned when an issue spontaneously arose from her childhood about her parents. She denied it. "But I love my parents. They were good to me. Everything was fine." As the months passed, she slowly began to accept the fact that everything was *not* fine, that she was deeply wounded. As time passed, she began to forgive her parents from her heart and the unconscious distance she had placed between her parents and herself disappeared.

In our last session, her face was rosy, her eyes were bright, and there was a joy and peace radiating from her. "Now," I told her, "your face proclaims the gospel message without your ever having to say a word. Your face tells all that the Kingdom of God has touched your heart."

It is true, as Jesus said, we are weary and find life burdensome. But, this too can be a blessing. If we accept our incompleteness and pain, it will make us pilgrims on a journey. No doubt we will come upon many wrong paths and dead ends. What we think will bring us happiness and peace does not. In the end, we will alight on what our hearts desire.

This final rest is not simply the absence of conflict. We sometimes believe that if all the people who annoy us and all of life's hardships were taken away, we would live in peace. We think the peace of the monastery is simply because it is removed from the stresses of everyday life. But only to remove these things would leave a void and a feeling of emptiness more terrible than the pain. Rather, this rest is a positive presence, a presence that radiates warmth and light. The alcoholic woman found for herself a sense of well-being, contentment, and peace. She found it in church on her knees. This light can only be the presence of God.

In Jesus, this light of God has already come to us. In him, this radiant glow lights up our world. But we do not see the light until we first feel the darkness. We cannot know its joy until we first know its absence in pain.

The young woman knew her alcoholic misery and reached out to the light. Joyce, too, faced her pain and opened her heart to these healing rays of God. We are as unhappy and addicted to our unhappiness as they were. It is only when our addictions no longer assuage our pain and we "hit bottom," as every addict does, that we can let go of everything to reach out for the one source of rest.

Although it frightens us to step into the darkness, the pain will propel us forward. Although we cannot see or touch God, we faintly hear a voice speaking to us, touching the deepest chord of our being, one that no one else can reach. The harmonious resonance that begins assures us, "Come to me, all you who are weary and find life burdensome, and I will give you rest."

# 4

# The Kingdom Is Now

ཟ❧ We often become discouraged in our prayer. We ask and ask and ask and it seems like no one is listening. We hear from childhood about a God who loves us and answers our prayers, but the reality appears much different. Few, if any, of our requests are answered and rarely in the way we desire. God is either asleep or impervious to our pleas!

The entire church is in a similar quandry. Christ promised to return soon to save his disciples in the last and definitive act of God. With confidence in God's promise, the church prays without ceasing for this glorious day: "Thy Kingdom come." And yet, 2,000 years later, the consummation of this Kingdom has *not* come. The atheist as well as the believer are justified in raising their voices and asking, "Where is God?"

Similarly, a young priest came to me recently to complain. Three times in his life, he said, he had experienced the Lord's presence in prayer. Each had been a wonderful encounter. He was filled with joy, warmth, and peace. He continues to pray for God to touch his life again but to no avail. "It feels like I am standing next to a closed door which only God can open from the other side. I can only stand here and wait."

Jesus told his disciples a parable about prayer. A widow wore out a corrupt judge with her constant requests. Finally, the judge said, "I care little for God or [people], but this widow is wearing me out. I am going to settle in her favor" (Lk 18:4b-5). Likewise, in Luke 11:8, we hear a related parable about a man who comes to a friend in the middle of the night and asks for three loaves of bread. The master of the house is reluctant at such an hour. However, the narrator says, "Though he does not get up and take care of the man because of friendship, he will do so because of his persistence, and give him as much as he needs."

Very often these parables are invoked to justify the need for persevering prayer. The homilist will say, "We should be like that friend at night or the widow, constantly beseeching God. Finally, he will answer us." But something is not quite right about such interpretations. We have an intuition that something important has been missed.

Are we to compare our loving God with a lazy friend or a corrupt judge? Do we have to repeat our requests day and night for him to hear us? Luke himself rejects such an interpretation, "If you, with all your sins, know how to give your children good things, how much more will the heavenly Father give the Holy Spirit to those who ask him" (Lk 11:13)? And again, "Will not God do justice to his chosen...will he delay long over them...? I tell you, he will give them swift justice" (Lk 18:7-8).

The point of the parables is precisely that God is not a lazy friend or a corrupt judge. The key is not in comparison but in contrast. If the corrupt judge and the lazy friend respond to pleas, how much more will Jesus' heavenly Father! Luke emphasizes not only that he will come, but that he will come swiftly.

This throws us back to our original conflict. If God answers swiftly, why does that priest stand by the door and wait for God to open? Why does not God simply open the door and let him come in? My response to the young priest took him by surprise. "God is not on the other side of the door," I explained. "On the other side is only your attachment to his gifts of warmth and peace. Rather, look for him on this side. He waits *with* you."

When we experience God's gifts of warmth and peace in prayer, we are overwhelmed by his power. We feel beautiful and holy. We cannot imagine anything more wonderful than such a heavenly feeling. "This," we think to ourselves, "is really God's complete presence. This is what I have been looking for." So, like thirsty people crazed for a drink of water, we desperately seek out this consolation.

Certainly, living in the presence of God brings such joy and peace. It is good to long for such a day. But now, in the age between the two comings of Christ, there may be a way to bring us closer to God. There may be a consciousness that gives a stronger witness that we have become one with him.

Psalm 121 tells us about God's consciousness in human terms. It says that the Guardian of Israel neither sleeps nor slumbers (v.4). He is totally and perpetually awake, keeping watch. For him, "a thousand years...are as a watch of the night" (Ps 90:4). He waits beyond time.

In his experience of the divine at the burning bush, Moses asked God his name. The response was, "I am who am" (Ex 3:14). Several times according to the gospel of

John, the divinity of Jesus is proclaimed by his citing the phrase, "I am." For example, "I solemnly declare it: Before Abraham came to be, *I am*" (8:58).

Our loving Father is the complete, dynamic, and simple act of being. "I am." But many times we are not like God in this respect. It has been said that the average conscious mind spends about 75% of its time on past events, 21% on future events, and only 4% on the present. The problem is that the past and the future do not exist. We have only the present.

An Asian student once asked his guru, "Master, what is the difference between you and me?" The master replied, "When I eat, I eat. When I walk, I walk. When I sit, I sit. You do none of these things." The key to enlightenment, according to the master, was to remain totally in the present. Because the student was not strong in spirit and could not, his heart and mind wandered.

God is the perfect act of being, perpetually present and always awake. Spiritual masters describe God as living completely in the "now." When we live in the present, we are present to him. When we are present to ourselves, our world, and others, we find his presence as well. If we grasp for something not really present behind some imaginary door, as did the young priest, it can only end in frustration. But if we have the courage to experience the present, we will find God, who is on our side of the door.

However, it is not so easy. To live in the present means opening ourselves to life at its fullest. To experience joy and pain, hope and sorrow without any shields protecting our emotions and our consciousness would be more than we could endure. We put blinders on our eyes, cotton in our ears, and a protective coating around our hearts to shield ourselves from the raw fury of life. Thus we miss much of life, much of ourselves, and much of God.

To that young priest and to all of us, God is not "out there," he is here. It is not he who eludes us, but we who cannot yet stand his presence. Do you not remember the message of Jesus: "The Kingdom of God is at hand"? He is on this side of the door. When we refocus our gaze from "there" to "here," then we will know him.

This, too, is not so easy. To find God, we must become like God. Instead of grasping for the future, we are to wait in the present. We are to live where he lives, in the "now." Thus we are to begin the everlasting vigil, to watch with him through the eternal night.

The psalmist said to God, "To finish the race I must become eternal like you." As we keep vigil, we slowly wake from our deadly sleep. Our eyes and ears open; we wake up. When we are truly awake we become aware of another presence; from him there is a radiant smile and a tender touch. He has been here with us all along. He has waited with us; he has waited for us. We have become eternal with him and we smile.

# 5

## The Kingdom Is Here

ॐ My father once asked, "If the Good Lord wants everyone to believe in him, why doesn't he just do something miraculous that everyone can see? Why doesn't he show himself so that everyone will believe in him?" My father is not a stupid man. This is a good question. Another way of phrasing the inquiry is: "If Jesus ushered in the Kingdom of God, where is it?"

The most obvious response is the words of Jesus himself, "My kingdom does not belong to this world" (Jn 18:36). Initially, we may think that Jesus is referring to a kingdom that is somewhere else, a far distant place we usually call "heaven." However, "heaven" is a Matthean euphemism for God. The proper name for God was not used in Jewish speech or writing because it was considered too sacred. "Heaven" is not properly a place but rather a person; it is God's very self.

It is true that Jesus' Kingdom, this presence of God or "heaven," is not of this world of flesh and matter. But neither is it a far-off place. Rather, as he himself said, "The reign of God is already in your midst" (Lk 17:21). He speaks this of himself, the embodiment of the Kingdom—he is among us. He also speaks of that divine presence spreading into all of creation and now becoming part of each of us, the body of Christ (1 Cor 12:27).

The Kingdom, this "heaven," is here in an incomplete and hidden way, yet it is here. The problem is that we have "eyes but no sight, ears but no hearing" (Mk 8:18). One senses Jesus' frustration with the stubbornness of those around him: "If you know how to interpret the look of the sky, can you not read the signs of the times" (Mt 16:3)? Jesus experienced this Kingdom; he was the Kingdom. But they did not see it, and they did not see him.

A television talk show host asked Mother Teresa, the well-known founder of the Missionaries of Charity, "Mother, how can you live and work among those wretched, dying people on the streets of Calcutta? There is so much filth, dirt, disease, and poverty." She responded, "Are they like that? I didn't know. All I know is that every morning I receive Jesus in the Eucharist and pray before him in the tabernacle. Then, everywhere I go, I see the same face of Christ." The saint sees the Kingdom; the other finds only a wretched humanity.

Mother Teresa sees a beauty in the midst of misery. Indeed, something new and wonderful is happening in all of creation, even, or I should say, especially, in the slums of Calcutta. It is being shot through with the life and presence of God. As Gerard Manley Hopkins wrote, "The world is

charged with the grandeur of God. It will flame out, like
shining from shook foil."[1] God's very self is being revealed; this Kingdom is breaking out in our world. Can
you not see it?

Jesus' complaint against the religious people of his day
was not that they were disobeying their religious rules; indeed, they scrupulously kept them. Rather, they were
blind guides (Mt 23:16, 24). But Jesus was not referring to
their physical eyes and ears. Obviously, they could see him
and hear him. Instead, he was referring to their deeper,
spiritual senses; these were shut tight.

Even today, it is not enough for a religious leader to use
gospel phrases and to have a kind demeanor. To spread the
Good News necessitates that we really perceive the Kingdom of God among us. We are to be aware of this presence
of God, this "heaven" on earth, and to proclaim it. If we are
not aware of it, we are "blind." And, as Jesus pointed out, a
blind guide can only lead another into the pit (Mt 15:14).

To see and hear the Kingdom, we need to wake up, to
rouse ourselves from the sleep of death, and to take on a
whole new vision. This complete, inner transformation is
alluded to in the epistle to the Ephesians. We are exorted
to "put on that new [person]" and to acquire a "fresh, spiritual way of thinking" (4:24, 23). In the gospel of John, Jesus admonishes Nicodemus that he must be "born again"
or "begotten from above" (3:4, 3). Christianity does not require a minor adjustment here and there; it calls for a complete rebirth.

Each one of us has a "horizon of consciousness," or a
personal lens, through which we experience life. For example, it is like wearing a pair of blue sunglasses—all of life
would appear to be blue. How we experience life depends
as much or more upon our lens/consciousness than it does
upon the reality of life itself.

Fr. Frank McNulty of the Catholic Archdiocese of New-
ark, New Jersey, tells the story of two priests who recently
were preparing for retirement. They had been classmates in

the seminary and had similar assignments throughout their careers. There was little to distinguish their ministerial lives. As Fr. McNulty spoke to each one, however, a very different picture began to emerge. The first spoke of the many wonderful people he had known. Life had been good to him and he wished he could do it all over again. He had found ministry life-giving and he was grateful. The second priest was bitter. He spoke with anger about his life and wanted to convey to the diocesan officials exactly what he thought of the priesthood. He could not wait to get out.

It would be an understatement to say that the horizon of consciousness of each priest was different. No doubt, too, the message they proclaimed during their ministries was also different. Is there any way that an angry priest can proclaim the Kingdom's message of joy and peace? Can a grateful one fail to be a living witness to the presence of God? How different their seemingly similar lives turned out!

We should not be surprised. Jesus said that in the end there would only be two groups. We will find ourselves on his right hand or his left. We will be sheep or goats, wheat or weeds, wise or foolish virgins.

Some will find the Kingdom, this "heaven," and know its peace; others will fashion for themselves an angry and bitter hell. We will not have to wait. Just as the Kingdom of God has already begun, so too with the realm of darkness. People are already constructing the abode of hell and sitting in its rage.

And so, Dad, to answer your question, the Kingdom is here. We cannot see it with our physical eyes because it is not of this world of flesh. But, it is here and our vocation is to learn to see it with our hearts. If we do, the words of Jesus will be words addressed to us: "Blest are the eyes that see what you see. I tell you, many prophets and kings wished to see what you see but did not see it, and to hear what you hear but did not hear it" (Lk 10:23-24).

My Dad and I join in this prayer: "May the Good Lord help us to see it!"

# Discussion Questions

1. Have I had an experience of God in my life? Has the Kingdom of God touched me?

2. What are my unhealed pains? What are the ways I avoid feeling pain? How might I enter into these hurts so that I will experience the Kingdom more fully?

3. God is in the "now"; where are my thoughts and attention directed? What keeps me from living more fully, living in the present?

4. Do I see the Kingdom of God in this world? What are the signs I see that the Kingdom is here?

# HOW DO I GET
# TO THE KINGDOM?

# 6

# We Think We Know

❧ The gospel seems reasonable to us. We are familiar with the sayings and teachings of Jesus and accept his message. We believe that our real challenge is not understanding, but simply living in accord with this message. I find this perspective to be frightening. If the message of Jesus appears easy to comprehend and accept, then perhaps it is not his message that we are being given at all.

The response of the people of Israel to this man was extreme. Some gave up everything they had to follow him. People flocked from all corners of the land to see him and touch him. He was hemmed in on every side and hounded day and night. The sick, the blind, and the lame cried out, "Son of David, have pity on us" (Mt 9:27).

He stunned the entire nation; the force and power of his message astounded his listeners. "He taught with authority and not like their Scribes" (Mt 7:29). He did not quote earlier rabbis and rabbinic traditions; he spoke directly from the Scriptures and from a personal awareness of God. Often he would say, "You have heard the commandment..." and "What I say to you is..." indicating a special authority whose source people did not know (Mt 5:21-22). They would question him about this authority but would not receive an answer they found sufficient (Mk 11:28).

Even his lifestyle was offensive. First of all, he did not marry. According to their Scriptures, it was God's will that a man should be married and rear children; those who did not were thought to be cursed. Not only did he not have a family, he even extolled his celibate life as an example: "And some there are who have freely renounced sex for the sake of God's reign" (Mt 19:12).

Second, he was the son of a carpenter and a carpenter himself. He was not a Levite nor did he come from the priestly tribe of Aaron. Likewise, he was not a rabbi and presumably had little formal training in Jewish tradition. At one point, "his large audience was amazed. They said: 'Where did he get all this?...Is this not the carpenter...?' " (Mk 6:2-3). It stunned the people and infuriated the priests to be taught about God by a carpenter. Indeed, "they found him too much for them" (Mk 6:2-3).

If the message that the "Kingdom of God is at hand" challenges the human heart, we would expect the bearer of the message to do the same. We are not disappointed. The people had such a hard time dealing with Jesus that they decided that "he is possessed by a devil—out of his mind" (Jn 10:20). At one point, even his own family came to take him home saying, "He is out of his mind" (Mk 3:21).

Initially, the authorities were merely interested and

they sent delegations to question him. As they became more skeptical, they tried to trip him up by asking questions that had no acceptable answer. To their surprise and eventual rage, he gave them one. Finally, they decided he must die so that the "whole nation" might not be "destroyed." (Jn 11:50).

The stories he told and the actions he performed are attractive to us. We think, "If I were alive 2,000 years ago, I would have followed him and rejoiced in him." I wonder. The stories he told were violently offensive to his audience. He consistently held up outcasts, the poor and powerless among them as examples to be followed. For example, "the Samaritans were a heretical and schismatic group...who were detested even more than pagans."[1] He told a story of a member of the hated Samaritans who helped a man who had been beaten and robbed. When he asked, "Which of these was neighbor to the man who fell in with the robbers?" they answered, "The one who treated him with compassion" (Lk 10:36-37). They could not even choke out the hated word, Samaritan. He could only call him "the one who."

Again, publicans, who collected taxes for the Roman government, were considered outcasts and were despised. Since they were Jews themselves, they were considered traitors. Not surprisingly, they were often dishonest as well. The phrase used for excommunication from the Jewish religious assembly was, "Treat him as you would a Gentile or a tax collector"[2] (Mt 18:17). Jesus' relationship with these people was inflammatory and it almost seems he was deliberately baiting them in his parables. He compared the prayer of one of their religious leaders, a Pharisee, to that of a sinner, a publican. He said the publican "went home from the temple justified but the other did not" (Lk 18:14). Could this have been anything but insulting to their religious sensitivities?

Even the parable that we find the most appealing, the prodigal son, was offensive to the Jews. The younger son squandered his money on dissolute living and ended up with an occupation that violated their religious sensitivities: a swineherd (Lk 15:11-32). Pigs were considered unclean and anyone who tended them became the lowest of humanity and ritually unclean. It would have been unthinkable for the prodigal's father not only to accept him back but to treat him with honor.

Time and again, Jesus championed the most despicable of society. He praised the Roman centurion for his faith: "I have never found this much faith in Israel" (Mt 8:10). He violated the Law of Moses and forgave the woman caught in the act of adultery (Jn 8:11). He ate with the uncircumcized; he spoke with Gentile women; he touched lepers—all violations of the Law, which made him impure. He even had the gall to chastise the righteous and tell them that "tax collectors and prostitutes are entering the Kingdom of God" before them (Mt 21:31b).

Jesus then directly assaulted their most sacred religious observances. He and his disciples did not follow the ritual washing of hands before a meal (Mt 15:2). He justified his actions by saying, "It is not what goes into a [person's] mouth that makes him impure; it is what comes out of his mouth" (Mt 15:11). He continually violated the sacred law of Sabbath rest. He healed on the Sabbath. He told a man to pick up his mat on the Sabbath. He allowed his disciples to pull off heads of grain on the Sabbath. Again, he justified his actions: "The sabbath was made for [people], not [people] for the sabbath. That is why the Son of Man is lord even of the sabbath" (Mk 2:27-28). At this point, even his disciples realized the gravity of his actions and cautioned him, "Do you realize the Pharisees were scandalized when they heard your pronouncement?" (Mt 15:12)

Finally, the words that alarmed the leaders the most was Jesus' statement, "The Father and I are one" (Jn 10:30). At that point, they picked up rocks to stone him. Jesus protested, "For which of these good deeds of mine do you stone me?" They replied, "It is not for any 'good deed' but

for blaspheming. You who are only a man are making
yourself God" (Jn 10:30-33). Their feelings were captured
in their response to a later discourse: "This sort of talk is
hard to endure" (Jn 6:60).

Much of the reason we do not find his words so obnox-
ious is because we are not his contemporary in ancient Pal-
estine. The Samaritans are not our enemies, nor are the Romans. We do not see tax collectors, swineherds, and
prostitutes outside of God's loving protection. The Pharisees' laws regarding the Sabbath and ritual worship are for-
eign to us and seem absurd. And we easily mouth the teaching that Jesus is truly God and man.

But if we have lost the context of Jesus' life, we are in
danger of losing his message. Thomas Merton lived a life
radically dedicated to the gospel in a Trappist monastery.
Only one week before the end of his life, he underwent a
powerful experience of the divine. "I was suddenly, almost
forcibly, jerked clean out of the habitual, half-tied vision of
things."[3] It took him a lifetime to come to this point. I fear
that we have not yet made it.

We *think* we see—a most dangerous perspective. As Jesus told the leaders, "If you were blind there would be no
sin in that. 'But we see,' you say, and your sin remains" (Jn
9:41).

# 7

# A Fire on the Earth

ᏊᎬ The image of Jesus popular today is that of a kind man who urged peace and reconciliation. He told us of the Father's love and he brought love and healing everywhere. This is certainly true of Jesus, but is it the whole picture?

A psychologist would tell us that the human mind does not rest for long in a state of "cognitive dissonance." This is where the mind is presented with contradictory understandings and struggles to make sense of the conflicting situation. It is a painful state to be in, but one that can foster growth and, indeed, an expansion of our horizon of consciousness.

The Jesus who spoke of love and peace also said, "I have come to light a fire on the earth. How I wish the blaze were ignited! I have a baptism to receive. What anguish I feel till it is over! Do you think I have come to establish peace on the earth? I assure you, the contrary is true; I have come for division" (Lk 12:49-51).

Because of the uncomfortable feeling of cognitive dissonance, such passages are rarely quoted. In fact, we are so selective in the picture we paint of Jesus that many may not even be aware that such passages exist. Instead of a warm and compassionate Jesus who speaks of the Father's forgiveness to the prodigal son, we are now faced with a radical Jesus who has come to light a "fire on the earth."

Jesus was not the first to use such images of God's word. The prophet Jeremiah received the word of God: "See, I place my words in your mouth" (Jer 1:9b). It was a difficult word that caused him much persecution as he preached against his beloved city of Jerusalem. He came to rue the day he was born and, in a heartfelt revelation, he tried to forget this word that had been given to him: "I say to myself, I will not mention him, I will speak in his name no more. But then it becomes like fire burning in my heart, imprisoned in my bones" (20:9).

The prophet Amos used similar imagery for the word of the Lord that came to him. First, Amos protested that he was not a professional prophet, but only a "shepherd and a dresser of sycamores" (Am 7:14). Then something startling happened to this man who tended fig trees and guarded sheep. The power of God touched his life: "Now hear the word of the Lord" (7:16)! For Amos, this experience was overwhelming and the image he used is as dramatic as it is colorful: "The lion roars—who will not be afraid! The Lord God speaks—who will not prophesy" (3:8)!

The word of God is like a fire in the heart: powerful, compelling, and carrying with it a force unknown to the

human consciousness. It is a fire on the earth that must
and will be enkindled.

Every day this fire is spread. This morning a woman in
her sixties told me of an overwhelming experience the
night before. For the first time, she decided to attend a
healing service conducted by a well-known priest gifted
with a special presence of the Holy Spirit. As she sat in the
pew, she was astounded to watch people walk up to receive a blessing. One after another "rested in the Spirit"
and fell gently to the floor. Though very nervous and
frightened, she decided to walk up herself and ask for a
blessing. She thought, "This can't happen to me. I don't believe what is going on. But whatever the Lord wants to
happen, let it be."

When the priest laid his hands on her head, she was
overcome with a sense of joy and peace she had never before experienced. She, too, gently fell to the floor and rested in an indescribable sense of God's loving presence. "Before," she said, "I would go to church on Sunday and
thought I believed. I never realized this was available. At
my age! I want to tell everyone about it. I want to tell them
to come. It will change their lives."

Indeed, it will. Whenever the Kingdom of God touches
our lives we are profoundly affected and converted. See
how on fire with the message she is. She wants everyone to
know about it, she wants everyone to come to the service.
Normally, she is a quiet, pleasant person. But when she
speaks of this experience, she is filled with enthusiasm; she
is on fire with the Holy Spirit. There is a sense of urgency
in her voice. It is as if she is saying, "Time is short. Hurry.
This is too important to be missed." There was a similar
sense of urgency in Paul. "I tell you, time is short...for the
world as we know it is passing away" (1 Cor 7:29, 31).

Scripture scholars tell us that the early church, and perhaps even Jesus himself, believed that the end of the
world was coming soon, so much so that at one point
Paul had to admonish the early Christians that they

should not quit working, and just sit and wait for the second coming of Christ. Unfortunately, in their view, these hopes were not realized.

But we are not to go back to our lives as they were before the Kingdom touched them, as the apostles did after Jesus' death. They went back to fishing, as if a hope-filled dream had been shattered. No, our sense of urgency, our sense of enthusiasm comes not from a proximity of the second coming, but from a power and presence that even now is having a profound effect. As Paul said, the world as we know it is passing away; it is being reformed and refashioned. The Word of God is among us, "making all things new" (Rv 21:5).

This is the flame that causes division. The woman who "rested in the Spirit" walked out of the church and was greeted by her skeptical husband. He poked fun at the service and expected his normally docile wife to demur. To his surprise, she gave him a dressing-down. Such a fire must be proclaimed, as Jeremiah testified.

Can the same Jesus who gave us the gift of peace also cause division? To us, peace and division are mutually exclusive; one cannot exist with the other. But in the gospel, peace is not an absence of conflict, but the dynamic presence of the Kingdom. Such a presence not only brings peace of heart but also a flame.

It is as if the whole world were a dry forest, waiting to ignite. And then, there is a *spark*! The divine presence ignites the world and it erupts into flame. Those who accept the spark find peace; those who reject it feel an internal division and will be swallowed up by the flames.

There is a fire on the earth. It is ignited by the Word of God and is spreading like a wild fire throughout creation. It is waiting to be enkindled in your hearts. Time is short. Do not wait. Repent and believe that the Kingdom of God is at hand.

# 8

# Repent, the Kingdom of God Is at Hand

&❧ I recently presided at a young woman's funeral. A heroin addict, she had finally succumbed through an overdose. During the eulogy, I spoke of her human weakness. She had, indeed, been painfully aware of her addiction and struggled hard to rid herself of it. She had, before her addiction, been a loving and caring person throughout, yet she could not overcome it.

The family could not accept her addiction or her failure to conquer it. They did not understand that it was a human

weakness so overpowering that she was emotionally para-
lyzed by it. She was fundamentally a strong and good person, they said, and they would rather not discuss it with
her or even think about it. Thus, she had been isolated in
her struggle from the very support she needed. That may
be one more reason why it finally killed her.

We do not like to admit weakness nor even our mortali-
ty. "Christians," we rationalize, "are strong people who
have no faults, no weaknesses, no sins."

How ironic! The Kingdom of God is a paradox. "The
first shall come last and the last shall come first" (Mk
10:31). "Unless you change and become like little children,
you will not enter the Kingdom" (Mt 18:3). "Let me make
it clear that tax collectors and prostitutes are entering the
Kingdom of God before you" (Mt 21:31b). This radical
Kingdom keeps destroying all of our preconceived no-
tions about the way things should be. We prepare for the
Kingdom, not by ignoring our weaknesses, but by facing
them squarely.

John the Baptizer prepared the people for the coming of
the Kingdom. As the precursor to the God-man, he insisted
on one act as the key to allowing this Kingdom to come:
"Reform your lives! The Reign of God is at hand" (Mt 3:2).
He wanted us to repent and to face our sins. Extolling our
virtues will not help; rather, we prepare for the Kingdom
by acknowledging our weaknesses.

I hear so many confessions that go something like this:
"Bless me, Father, for I have sinned. My last confession
was one year ago. Since then I have missed Mass once and
had several impure thoughts. That is all." I feel like
screaming, "You've lived an entire year and that is all? I'll
bet if I asked your spouse what your sins are, I'd hear a
long list."

Which one of us is not envious of others? Who is not
filled with pride and self-sufficiency? Who does not treat
others with coldness or hostility? Is there anyone who does
not judge others or malign their characters?

What scares me the most is not that we are committing serious offenses—humankind has always done so and always will—but that we are not aware of them. We are like dumb animals being led to the slaughter thinking that we are going to a feast. This is the nature of sin. It blinds us to the truth about ourselves and puts us to sleep—a comfortable, deadening, and most deadly sleep.

In contrast, the desert prophet, the man with a leather belt around his waist who fed on grasshoppers and wild honey, called us to wake up. Time is short! The Kingdom is on the verge of breaking into our world. Repent, confess your sins before it is too late....

People hate to hear this because it smacks of over-zealous preachers who pound home a message of sin and damnation. Instead of feeling liberated, people are oppressed. The result is that we rarely hear about sin. The overdone message of "love, love, love" prompted one parishioner to utter, "If I hear one more sermon on love I am going to leave the church." Unfortunately, neither the "sin, sin, sin" approach nor the "love, love, love" sermons hasten the arrival of the Kingdom. The former instills only fear, guilt, and anger; the latter puts us all to sleep to the true nature of a society ripped apart by division and strife.

Both approaches lack one essential ingredient. Though they speak an important element in the gospel message, they do not touch people's hearts. Something is lacking: a personal experience of the Kingdom. "Love" means nothing to someone who has never felt love. The darkness of sin means nothing to a person who does not know the light of grace. The warmth of love and the light of grace are both experiences of the Kingdom.

Ironically, it has always been the greatest of saints who have confessed themselves to be the greatest of sinners. How many saints have spent long periods lamenting their sins and asking for mercy! We think this is the pious exaggeration of rather peculiar people. "Surely, they are not such outrageous sinners," we say.

If this were true, then their attitude would be a false humility. But true humility, and thus sanctity, admits only the truth. We are left with a contradiction. If these people were such great saints and they confessed themselves to be wretched sinners, were they telling the truth? Of course, they were. The further we go into the heart of the Kingdom, the more the light of grace illumines our lives; thus, the more we see. Compared to the power and purity of such a tremendous light of grace, we are indeed wretched sinners. The saints were aware of this because they knew the Kingdom. We are not aware. This should frighten us.

Paradoxically, our sins and weaknesses are doors for the Kingdom to enter. The people who consider themselves to be whole and self-sufficient have no need of salvation, no need of the Kingdom. But weaknesses are like openings for another to enter. They entice a compassionate heart to seek out that which is lost, to heal the broken-hearted, to bind up the wounded spirit.

Speaking of the sin of humanity, the Easter proclamation exults, "O happy fault, O necessary sin of Adam." It was this fault that brought us such a wonderful savior. I know of an alcoholic who has been in Alcoholics Anonymous for many years. He has come, after years of sobriety, to view his disease of alcoholism as a blessing. Because he was brought low, he came to recognize his human weakness and his need for God. He said, "I feel sorry for those who do not have such a disease and thus do not know their need for God." His alcoholism was a door for the Kingdom to enter.

The problem today is not that we reject Jesus as our savior. Everyone will nod in assent to this. The difficulty is that we do not feel the need for such salvation. As Revelation points out, "You keep saying, 'I am so rich and secure that I want for nothing.' Little do you realize how wretched you are, how pitiable and poor, how blind and naked" (Rv 3:17)!

Thomas Merton gave us an appropriate image: We imagine that we are drowning and God is reaching out to us at the last moment. On our third and last time as we descend into the water to a certain death, God reaches out and pulls us to safety. That is salvation!

Unfortunately, we do not know we are drowning. We do not experience a personal need for help. We are not aware of our weaknesses and thus there are no doors for the Kingdom. To use a gospel phrase, "We are dead in sin" (Eph 2:5).

Should sin be preached more? I think not, it would only make people feel guilty. Should we preach only the love of God? This denies the fundamental brokenness we all experience and of which we are subconsciously aware. Neither seems to touch the core of the human heart.

What should we do? We cannot force God to shed the light of his Kingdom, though I believe he does so abundantly. Nor can we force people to look at something about themselves that they cannot face.

Perhaps, as a first step, we can pray for the light to accept the truth, as painful as it is. We can tell people that there is no other way, no shortcut, no easier road to peace than this awareness that we are sinners in need of salvation. Even today, we hear the words of John the Baptizer ringing in our hearts, "Repent, for the Kingdom of God is at hand."

# 9

# Choose Life

&⁂  There is a tendency in society to believe that every-one will go to "heaven" after death. The rationale goes something like this: "God loves all of us so much he couldn't possibly send anyone to hell." It is perhaps no coincidence that the generation that has problems acknowledging the reality of personal sin also has difficulties believing in the possibility of an estrangement from God.

The first part of the statement is clearly true, "God loves all of us." But the second part can be confusing: "God couldn't possibly send anyone to hell." Our society rejects the image of a harsh, angry God, which, fortunately, Jesus himself rejected: "I do not come to condemn the world but to save it" (Jn 12:47). Indeed, God does not condemn anyone.

There is, however, an alternative that has not yet been considered. Although God sends no one to hell, perhaps people freely walk through the gates of perdition. They freely choose to reject the Truth and insist on their own damnation. The scenario might go as follows:

> God says, "Come to my house." We say, "No, I am afraid. I don't trust you." God says, "You do not understand. You will be happy with me." We insist, "No, I hate it. It will hurt me." God pleads, "Please, trust me. You can only find peace here. The gates of paradise are wide open to you." We conclude, "You are trying to kill me. I refuse."

It is a short, one-act play dramatizing the reality of human choice. God is not the cause of our damnation; we who choose it are. The gates of heaven are wide open to all and Jesus stands at the gate with open arms waiting for each of us. He promised that "in my Father's house there are many dwelling places" and that he is "going to prepare a place" for us (Jn 14:2). Unfortunately, some of us take up a different abode.

The real mystery is why we reject it. It is clear, as St. Augustine says, that "We were made for thee, O Lord, and our hearts are restless until they rest in thee." There can be no peace and happiness apart from God. To reject God is to reject any possibility for a fulfilling life and the possibility of eternal bliss.

But look around you. Just as there are signs of the Kingdom of God everywhere, there are also signs of the reign of darkness. Do you reject the reality of sin? Take another look. There are wars in every part of the globe. Entire nations are starving while others are overweight. The world is wounded by injustice, hatred, abortion, infanticide, ra-

cism, murder, sexual abuse, and rape. We proclaim with
Jesus that the Kingdom of God is at hand! Horribly, the
reign of death is also present.

Perhaps this is the reason for the urgency and immedia-
cy of Jesus' message: You do have a choice. What you
choose will be of ultimate importance for you and the
world. Make haste. Do not delay.

Do you find it hard to imagine that someone would not
choose God? Unfortunately, experience tells us otherwise. I
painfully remember an elderly man, a regular church-goer,
who became more and more angry with life. He was mad
at the world. His landlord was unfair. He hated people
making noise before church services. He was angry at his
family and stopped seeing them. He was filled with a rage
that blinded him to any goodness. It was impossible to talk
to him. Ministers tried to reach him but without success.
Sadly, his life was drawing to a close in self-imposed isola-
tion and rage. Despite his religiosity, I fear for him. We
commend him to the power of God's mercy and love.

Some people hope for a deathbed conversion. This is
possible...I remember a friend who was outraged at the
idea of such a "cheap" way to get into heaven. He thought
it was so unfair. "Someone could lead a life of evil and,
then, at the last minute confess his sins and end up in
heaven, just like the rest of us."

First of all, anyone who lives a life of evil already re-
ceives the misery that evil brings. Sin is not fun. Second,
there is a striking similarity between his attitude and that
of the elder brother's in the parable of the prodigal son.
Likewise, it reminds one of a second parable concerning
the workers in the vineyard. They complained that they
had worked a full day in the scorching heat and had been
paid the same as those who had worked only an hour. The
Master himself chastised their narrow hearts: "Are you envious because I am generous" (Mt 20:15)?

However, there is a condition for a deathbed conversion.
It has to be a true change of heart, a real conversion. If

someone were to live an intentional life of evil and then, wishing to escape eternal retribution, were to say, "I choose Jesus," would that be a true conversion? Clearly not.

In fact, that last attempt to escape retribution is just another selfish act that finishes off a lifetime of self-centered actions. He is not really choosing Jesus. He uses the word, "Jesus," but he is really choosing his false self...again. There is no conversion and there is no life.

It is hard to change a lifetime of either goodness or evil, even at the end. A popular theory today is the "final option." Some theologians believe that at our deaths, we will see God and be given one, final, clear choice. I believe it. However, the more we follow one path, good or evil, the more entrenched we become. We become what we love and it is hard to change our very being.

The choices we make are not merely notional ones that do not affect us. Rather, they are transforming choices. The people who choose the Kingdom of God become more joy-filled, more peaceful, full of light, full of God. The Kingdom is their natural home. Those who choose darkness slowly become angry, bitter, resentful, hateful, envious, spiteful. They become beasts, devils.

The choice for the reign of darkness is initially easy. It is full of sensual enticement and illusory promises of happiness to come. The choice for God's Kingdom is initially a difficult struggle. Jesus said, "How narrow is the gate that leads to life, how rough the road, and how few there are who find it" (Mt 8:14)!

Because of original sin, the wounding of human nature that was created "very good," we have developed an attraction to evil, a craving for the darkness. We need to retrain ourselves and rediscover our love of goodness. Through a life of prayer, penance, faith, and charitable works, we learn to love goodness and to develop a "taste" for the Kingdom of God. It is a slow and painful process. Yet, there are many moments when the joy and light of this Kingdom break into our hearts. These moments spur us on the rough path and provide encouragement to flagging hearts.

It is awesome to realize that it is we who choose to be full of grace or evil. It is we who choose to find heaven on this earth or to fashion a hell for ourselves. We, alone, will allow ourselves to be transformed into beings of light or to wear, eternally, the mask of a beast.

Jesus proclaimed the message with urgency. Wake up. Time is short. Choose now. What you choose now will change you and, if it takes you down the wrong path, each passing day will make it harder to turn back. And who knows the day or the hour when the Master will return? That day will come like a "thief in the night" (1 Thes 5:2).

The Book of Deuteronomy, long before the time of Jesus, prophetically proclaimed the truth: "I have set before you life and death, the blessing and the curse. Choose life, then, that you and your descendants may live" (30:19).

# 10

## Accept the Gift

৵  In the gospel of Luke, there is the well-known story of Zacchaeus, a tax collector. Because he is a "man of short stature," when he hears that Jesus is coming he climbs a tree to see him. Jesus approaches Zacchaeus and tells him that he plans to stay at his house. The crowd objects, "He has gone to a sinner's house"—something forbidden to a righteous Jew. Zacchaeus then defends himself, "I give half my belongings, Lord, to the poor. If I have defrauded anyone in the least, I pay him back fourfold." Jesus responds, "Today salvation has come to this house" (Lk 19:1-10).

The usual interpretation that one hears from pulpits and reads in Scripture commentaries is that Jesus' presence causes Zacchaeus to convert from his sinful ways; in the future, he says, he intends to help the poor and right injustices. However, this is not faithful to the text of the story. Zacchaeus's statement is in the present tense. He says, "I give" and "I pay him back." Zacchaeus is not changing his evil ways; he has always done such righteous deeds.[1]

The problem with this understanding is that the response of Jesus no longer makes any sense. If Zacchaeus has always done such good deeds, why would Jesus say, "Today salvation has come to this house"? What did Zacchaeus do that day to warrant salvation?

This last question reveals the root of the problem. We tend to think that in order for Jesus to declare that salvation has come to Zacchaeus, he must have done something to deserve it. Something in the core of our fallen being believes that we can and must, by our own efforts, do something to merit salvation. This is simply not true. The hardest lesson of life to grasp is that there is nothing we can do to *earn* salvation.

Try as we might, we constantly fall back into our own weaknesses and sins. In the confessional, people always lament that they confess the same sins. They are ashamed and discouraged: ashamed that the priest "has to hear" the same thing time and again, and discouraged that they have not overcome their weaknesses.

While it is true that we do make progress in overcoming our faults, the real progress in these people's confessions is of greater import. Time after time when we face the same human weaknesses in ourselves and realize that we are really powerless to eradicate them, we are led to the brink of despair. We think to ourselves, "There is no hope in me." Indeed, strictly speaking, there is no such hope.

At one point the disciples of Jesus came to such a point of despair. It seemed as if salvation were beyond them, as indeed it was. "They were completely overwhelmed, and exclaimed, 'Then who can be saved?'" Jesus responded, "For [human beings] it is impossible; but for God all things are possible" (Mt 19:25-26). Salvation is not an act of humankind; it is the work of God.

Unfortunately, it seems that few of us come to this brink of despair. How often people justify themselves by saying, "I'm a good person and don't do anything wrong," implying that they are righteous in God's sight. But if we were to judge by God's criteria, we might see things differently.

Jesus tells us what God expects: "When a person strikes you on the right cheek, turn and offer him the other. If anyone wants to go to law over your shirt, hand him your coat as well" (Mt 5:39-40). He says that it is not enough to love those who love you—the pagans do that much. "Love your enemies," he says. "Pray for your persecutors...you must be made perfect as your heavenly Father is perfect" (Mt 5:44, 48). Is there anyone among us who meets such exalted standards?

Zacchaeus did actually do something right. It was not his benevolence to the poor that brought salvation to his house. Rather, an offer was made that he "welcomed with delight": Jesus said he would come to his house; the very incarnation of salvation entered his life. In Jesus, salvation walked in through the front door.

It was not earned, though his just deeds did prepare Zacchaeus. He could not force salvation to come, though he sought it out by climbing a tree. And, when offered, he welcomed it with great joy. Salvation could not be coerced, yet it walked freely through his door.

An old priest told me that he often has moments when he is afraid that he will not be saved. Objectively speaking, there is no reason why he should not be saved; he has lived an exemplary life. However, he could sense that he cannot control God. He cannot grab onto God and ensure his salvation. The moment he reaches out, God seems to slip away.

In his old age—his health is slipping away; his friends

have all died and he is retired and alone— he would like to grab onto something that might anchor him. There is nothing to hope in and the future has only darkness and the void. "Even an old priest cannot capture and chain God to assuage his need to save himself," he said. "My entire life has been spent unconsciously trusting in my own religiousness. Now even that is gone."

The old priest was coming to that final point of surrender. There is nothing we can do or grab onto to save ourselves—not even our religious acts will save us. Salvation is simply and totally a free gift to be humbly accepted. To come to that point of awareness and self-surrender demands a lifelong stripping away of everything, even our own "piety." In the end, we let go into the darkness and void of death—trusting that God will be on the other side. It is as Jesus said, "Whoever would save his life will lose it, and whoever loses his life for my sake will save it" (Lk 9:24). It reminds me of an old story:

> A bishop dies and appears before St. Peter at the heavenly gates. The bishop asks what he has to do to pass through. Peter tells him it takes 100 points to get in. The bishop thinks to himself, "That should be easy, I have lived a model Christian life."
>
> So he says, "I have been a dedicated bishop all my life and cared for my flock with devotion."
>
> "Indeed," says Peter, "you were a model bishop and an example for all. That is seven points." The bishop is stunned that it only counted for seven points.
>
> "Well," says the Bishop, "I cared for my parents in their old age, never letting the slightest need go unmet. I was a model son."
>
> "Indeed," says Peter, "you were. That is four points." Not only is the bishop surprised at how little progress he is making, he is starting to panic that he might not make it into heaven.

Frantically, the bishop recounts each charitable deed of his life, all the time Peter is nodding his assent. Finally, when he concludes, Peter says he is only up to seventeen points, far short of the necessary 100.

In despair, the bishop throws up his hands and says, "I can't make it. I guess I'll just have to trust in the Lord." "Ah," says Peter, "that is 100 points!"

# 11

## Abandon Yourself to God

❧ Judy, a forty-eight year old woman, had a heart attack. Her future is unknown. She may have to undergo open heart surgery although, due to other complications, that might not be possible. Now she is confined to her home, unable to do anything but the most menial of tasks.

Judy is upset because she is afraid she is losing her faith. "All my life I have been a good Christian. I regularly attend worship services and pray daily. I used to feel as though I was a pretty good person. Now I am filled with anger and fear. I am afraid of what the future will bring and angry that this should happen to me while I am so young. It is so unfair."

When our life is going well, our emotions buoy up our faith and we spontaneously praise and thank God for our blessings. We feel safe; we feel holy; we believe ourselves to be truly Christian. Happiness and contentment are in harmony with our understanding of faith. But when life turns sour, we are naturally filled with hurt, fear, and anger. Are Christians allowed to feel such emotions? Do not the Scriptures say that "perfect love casts out all fear" (1 Jn 4:18)? Are we not admonished to get rid of all "passion, anger, and bitterness" (Eph 4:31)? No wonder Judy is afraid she is losing her faith.

She asked me, "Do you think God understands?" I responded, "I know that I understand why you are angry and frightened. If I can understand, how much more will God." At that point, she sat back and breathed a deep sigh.

Faith is more than an emotion. We have little or no control over our feelings. They come and go like the wind and, try as we might, we cannot make ourselves feel the way we want, nor can we dismiss a hurt or an emotion we do not like. We can bury it deep in our unconscious but it will wreak even more havoc there and have an even greater impact on us.

Much important work is being done today in the area of human emotions. There is no single development that has changed the direction of spirituality today more than the growth of psychology. Despite its great benefits, however, there is an undesirable tendency emerging: to make our emotions into monarchs, thus making us their slaves.

For example, human love is often believed to be purely an emotion. When our emotions are soft and warm we say that we love someone. The next day we may feel cold and angry toward that person and we believe that we do not love him or her anymore. Love, then, becomes a capricious and arbitrary master destroying the other's sense of security and acceptance.

St. Paul himself professes that through weathering hard times, he has come to move beyond such a capricious master. "I am experienced in being brought low, yet I know what it is to have an abundance. I have learned how to cope with every circumstance—how to eat well or go hungry, to be well provided for or do without. In him who is the source of my strength I have strength for everything" (Phil 4:12-13).

Regardless of circumstances, Paul has come to a certain equanimity. This is not to say that he did not feel the full gamut of powerful human emotions—his letters are full of them. Rather, beneath the joy and the pain, the happiness and the anger, was something more powerful and more sure. His was a house built on rock (Mt 7:24).

This rock, which is God, holds us steady when the winds of our emotions blow from one direction, then the next. Yet, there is one more human experience, a terrible one indeed, that threatens even this rock foundation and tries the stoutest of Christian hearts.

Helen was a seventy-year-old woman with lung cancer. One moment she was healthy and the next she was in bed with only weeks to live. The family was stunned. Helen faced the terrible spectre of death in its full force. On her death bed, she said, "I have to face it squarely. I have to stay ahead of it." Helen was a woman of courage and she faced death head on.

One day I received a call. "Helen needs you." I walked into her room and sat down. "Helen, how are you?" "Sometimes good," she responded, "but sometimes...." Her voice trailed off. "What happens the other times?" I asked, "Are they not so good?" "No," she said, "Not so good." "What is it like, then?" I asked. "It feels like God has abandoned me," she responded. "I'm sorry. It must be difficult," I said. "Yes," she said, as tears welled up in her eyes. "Helen, when you said it feels like God has abandoned you, what is that like?" She replied, "It feels like nothing...just nothing."

At the moment of death, the only anchor that a Christian can rely on is God. When God is not there, there is a mortal cry of anguish that rends the hardest of human hearts. It was the agony that resounded from the hill of Calvary, "My God, my God, why have you forsaken me" (Mk 15:34)? At that point there is nothing—no feeling of faith, no awareness of God's presence. It is a sense of complete emptiness, or, as Helen said, "It feels like nothing...just nothing."

The "mystical doctor," St. John of the Cross, coined a phrase for this experience, the "dark night of the soul." "Nothing can be compared to the [dark night of the soul], for it is horrible and frightful."[1] The holy person, who has come to rely only upon God, now feels that God has abandoned him.

Many casually use the phrase, "dark night of the soul," to describe any trial or suffering, but it actually refers to the most horrible of all, the one that Helen underwent. The only possible source of consolation and hope is gone. There is only nothingness. This pricks the most primal human fear. More than death itself, we fear the plunge into nothingness.

Theologians and spiritual writers offer many reasons to justify this experience. It strengthens the soul, they say, teaches it to rely on God alone, cleanses it from impurities and attachments to consolations. No doubt these are true, but in the midst of such terror they seem insignificant and shallow.

This terrible moment reveals the fundamental—the only—human choice we have in this life. Perhaps all our decisions are an acting out of this one choice: We either fall into a hopeless despair or rise in a pure act of faith.

The latter was Jesus' choice. Abandoned on the cross, he made such an act of faith, "Father, into your hands I commend my spirit" (Lk 23:46). The former choice reminds one of the sign over the gates of hell in Dante's inferno, "Abandon all hope, ye who enter here." Perhaps they are there because they have already done so.

The prospect of such a choice is tremendous, in the true sense of the word. It is brought on by an equally tremendous experience, a sense of being forsaken by God. More than an emotion, beyond an ability to pray, deeper than even the light of grace seems able to reach, there is complete darkness. Out of this darkness comes a faint voice; the soul utters a credo that has truly become its own, "I believe."

# 12

# Take Up Your Cross

🙠 No gospel phrase has been more maligned and misused than this: "Take up your cross and follow me" (see Mt 16:24, Lk 14:27, Mk 8:34). Whenever suffering, injustice, and oppression are justified as God's will that must be passively endured, Karl Marx's statement that "religion is the opiate of the people" is correct. The addictive opium "high," in this case, is the promise of a reward after death. Thus we become mindless sheep, accepting every outrage thrust upon us.

It is not God's will that suffering and death should be a

part of our world; they are the result of sin. Just as peace and joy are the natural fruits of the Kingdom of God, human suffering and death are the fruits of evil.

When Jesus came into this world of sin, he "did not come to condemn the world but to save it" (Jn 12:47). It is appropriate, therefore, that all of the miracles he performed were positive signs of the Kingdom—they brought healing and life. Never did he perform a miracle to condemn or to punish.

Francis is a middle-aged man who complains that a friend calls him on the phone constantly and talks for hours. Even when Francis finally says that he has to leave, his friend ignores him and keeps on talking. Francis confesses that his sin is one of anger—he is furious at his friend. I tell Francis that his real sin is not anger but cowardice. He has disguised his cowardice with a pious smile. He feels he is being very Christian by being so kind to his friend. Actually, his friend is manipulating and controlling him, which Francis accepts as his "cross."

If the truth be known, Francis simply does not have the courage to stop this neurotic aspect of their relationship. Not only is Francis's cowardice causing himself an internal rage, it is not helping his friend, either. Francis's timidity encourages his friend to continue his controlling behavior. In reality, Francis's "cross" is a self-inflicted wound.

Jesus did not commit suicide on the cross. Even at the end, he prayed, "If it is possible, let this cup pass me by" (Mt 26:39). Rather, the challenge of his message and the power of the Kingdom threatened the forces of evil and sin so fundamentally that they conspired to kill him. It is as if suffering and death's very existence were threatened by the healing touch of the doctor so, in a fury, they attacked him with their disease.

Something similar might have happened to Francis had he spoken the truth. If he had said, "Stop! You are hurting me and are making me angry. You ignore my pleas to end this conversation and disregard my feelings. Why do you treat me this way?" In response, his friend would likely become angry and lash out at Francis. He, too, would have tried to silence the voice that revealed his sin.

We have an idea that the cross of Jesus was redemptive; it saved humankind. Recently, some scholars have questioned whether Jesus went to his death willingly, suggesting it may have been forced upon him, that he went to Calvary "kicking and screaming." This is absurd. It implies that suffering in and of itself is salvific. It suggests that suffering is intrinsically good. This is not true; suffering is intrinsically evil.

In New Testament times, disease and demonic possession were often linked. Thus a man who was mute was thought to be "in the grip of the devil" (Acts 10:38). When "the devil was cast out the dumb man spoke" (Lk 11:14). With our medical sophistication, we reject such simplistic equations and we rightly see that the immediate cause of a disease or physical impairment is not sin but a virus, a chemical imbalance, or a genetic defect.

But if suffering and death are ultimately the result of sin, perhaps in some spiritual way, when we do suffer or die, we could be said to be in the grip of the devil. It is not God's will.

Actually, many people seem to become worse because of their suffering. They become more embittered, self-centered, and miserable. Have you ever heard someone constantly complain about what the world has done to him? Rather than being his salvation, the suffering has sped up his approaching death. It is so hard to witness the screaming death of a person who is overcome with fear and bitterness. The reality of hell no longer seems so absurd.

Jesus' suffering and death had a different quality to it. It was not forced upon him, nor did he seek it out; rather it was accepted. It appeared to be the destruction of all that he had worked for. Some of his disciples returned to fishing after this event; their hope was gone (Jn 21:3). But this death became Jesus' greatest work, his most surprising act, and his most profound miracle. He is delivered into the "hands of men" (Lk 9:44), who were acting under an evil influence and, therefore, Jesus was delivered into the hands of Satan. Thus, Jesus "descends into hell." Perhaps the dark angel believed that he had his greatest catch of all. No doubt, ultimate victory seemed to be his.

What happened at this point can only be described as a mystery. It reminds one of the joy that radiated from the face of Stephen as he was being stoned (Acts 6:15, 7:55) or the voices of the early Christians raised in song as they were being torn apart by lions. Perhaps you yourself have experienced some taste of this mystery? Many have said that in their darkest hour, in a personal crisis or a critical illness, a light shines in the center of their suffering heart. It is not just that God rescues the person from Satan and makes the light scatter the darkness. The miracle is greater than that. It is rather that the very act of suffering—Satan's "victory"—brings about the destruction of the powers of darkness. What was the instrument of evil, in a stunning reversal, becomes the instrument of God.

I do not understand it. Satan himself must have been enraged and the angels of God astounded. I have never read nor heard a good explanation of it. I do not think I ever will. That it is true is confirmed by what followed: the blinding light of the resurrection, the victory of God.

Nevertheless, we mortals are not to seek suffering and death; that would be to tempt God. Nor are we to see suffering as a sign of the Kingdom; it is not. But it will always be a sign that this life is not only touched by the Kingdom of God, but also wounded by the powers of darkness.

Christians everywhere are called to usher in the Kingdom of God with all their might. As Jesus healed, raised the dead, and called people to righteousness, so are we to fight disease and death, to right injustices, and to deliver from oppression.

Sadly, though, a day will come when all of us will be delivered into the "hands of men" and ultimately into the bowels of death. For many it will end there. Bishop Fulton Sheen lamented that much suffering in the world is wasted and ends merely in bitterness and death. Suffering is, and will always remain, the instrument of evil and the fetid fruit of sin.

Christianity is not a drug to anesthetize us to the pain of true suffering. Nor can we close our eyes to the real crosses of our lives in favor of more comfortable ones of our own choosing. We need only speak the truth in all its raw, challenging power and the "father of lies" will attack us in his fury (Jn 8:44).

Christianity propels us into the heart of the conflict to proclaim the option of life. Thus, like our Master, our "hour will come" when we are to take up our cross (Jn 12:23). If we undergo the trial with faith in a greater power, hope in him who has gone before us, and a self-sacrificing love, the mystery will be re-enacted. Jesus died as he lived; it was a pouring out of himself for those he loved. Thus for him, and hopefully for us, the cross will be transformed from an instrument of torture into the sign of the victory of life.

# 13

## The Truth Will Set You Free

ᘒ A friend of mine is an associate pastor in a large parish in another part of the country. There is one other associate and, of course, an old pastor. Unfortunately, the best thing one could say about the pastor is that he is mentally unstable. He daily lapses into fits of rage, screams at the staff and throws tantrums when things do not go his way. Smiling one minute, he will be overcome with a wave of bitterness and filth the next. In psychological terms, one would say that he has a serious personality disorder, perhaps a borderline personality. One could make a case for the man being possessed.

This pastor has been ruling that parish—he does indeed rule—for eleven years. Sometimes he gets his way with a superficial smile and the subtle threat of anger. At other times he controls people through his outbursts, which he justifies by others' "incompetence" and his "superiority." Deluded with grandeur and drunk with power, he manipulates and uses everyone to feed his ego.

The bishop refuses to do anything about it. Had the priest been mismanaging funds, caught in a sexually compromising situation, or arrested for drunkenness, the bishop would act. But what could he be expected to do about a pastor that people simply "didn't get along with"?

The parish staff and the parishoners feel powerless to challenge the deranged man. "Besides," many say, "he's not that bad. He has a few faults, but he does good things, too." Most feel it is not their problem and steer clear of him. As a result, collections are dwindling, attendance has dropped, and the parish is slowly dying.

Similar situations have affected all of us. Some work for a tyrant. Others are brought up in dysfunctional homes. Still others have friends, spouses, or children who are emotionally ill. Psychotics, alcoholics, physically and emotionally abusive people affect our lives in devastating ways. It is often estimated that one out of every ten people suffers from the disease of alcoholism. The percentage of children who are sexually abused is probably higher. No one escapes the effects of traumatic illness.

Lesser emotional illnesses, called neuroses, impact our lives in more subtle ways. Every person's psyche has been damaged by original and personal sins. We are then bruised and hurt by the people closest to us who are often not even aware of the harmfulness of their actions. For years we remain silent, most of the time not even willing to admit the problem to ourselves.

Growing up, most of us have heard the phrase, "If you

cannot say anything nice, do not say anything at all." Such polite behavior is socially acceptable. Christians often elevate this maxim to the status of a golden rule. We say that a true Christian is one who only says positive things about others. "My aunt was a saint," we hear; "she always said nice things."

In Matthew 23, Jesus does *not* say nice things. He calls some scribes and Pharisees a barrage of insulting names. He says they are "frauds" (v.13), "blind fools" (v. 17), "blind guides" (v. 24), "brood of serpents" (v. 33). Though they appear to be holy, Jesus says that they are "full of filth and dead men's bones" (v. 27).

When I am teaching a class at our middle school, I will often present a syllogism to our young students. I first ask them the major premise: "Is it always a sin to be angry?" They predictably answer yes. Then I ask them the minor premise: "Was Jesus ever angry?" If they are not sure, I quote Mark 3:5: "Jesus looked around at them with anger, for he was deeply grieved that they had closed their minds against him."

"If it is always a sin to be angry," I tell them, "and Jesus was angry, we must conclude that Jesus committed a sin. Right?" Unfortunately, they usually nod their heads in agreement. "Wrong!" I insist, "The gospels are clear. Jesus is a human being like us in all things except sin" (Heb 4:15, 1 Pt 2:22).

Of course, the error in the syllogism is in the major premise. It is not always a sin to be angry. Nor were the harsh words of Jesus to some scribes and Pharisees occasions of sin. Our Lord simply told them the truth. It was an act of charity. They were leading wicked lives and the only hope they had was to recognize the truth and to reform.

Time and again, well-intentioned people will ask me for help, explaining that a family member is callously causing them an enormous amount of hurt. It may be a demanding and thankless invalid, an adolescent who is completely out of control, or an abusive parent whose only words are sarcastic comments and belittling remarks. At the confrontation, the injured parties would seethe with anger and have great difficulty smiling at the perpetrator and acting as if nothing were wrong.

I try to help them to see that they are lying—in the way they act. They are pretending that un-Christian behavior is not taking place and their actions assent to the lie. Because they are not exposing the crime, they are a party to it. And the crime is as devastating to them as it is to the one who commits it.

People will then say, "I don't feel good about being angry" or "I do not want to get into an argument." But "feeling good" is not synonymous with being a Christian. Not being in arguments is also not a good measure of one's sanctity. The gospels chronicle Jesus' running conflict with the civil and religious authorities of his day, a conflict that eventually ended in violence.

Jesus valued something more than harmonious relations—the truth. He said there was only one way to freedom: "The truth will set you free" (Jn 8:32). Day in and day out he told the truth, praising people when their actions were good and condemning them when they were bad. He rejoiced at joyful news (Lk 10:21), wept in times of sorrow (Lk 19:41), and was angered by the hardness of their hearts (Mk 3:5). In every way, his reactions were totally and perfectly human. He was a person like us in all things except sin.

My friend, the associate pastor, recently told me that something has finally changed in his parish. On the feast of Pentecost, the parish staff gathered, while the deranged pastor was on vacation, to share their feelings. They began to realize what was happening to them and to their parish. In a moment of grace, their common feelings of confusion, hostility, and powerlessness were now revealed to be a result of the pastor's disease. The truth about the man's sickness came to light.

When the pastor came back, the entire staff sat down to

discuss the matter with him. Each one had a chance to tell his or her story. Firmly, yet with compassion, they told him the truth about himself. For three hours he was forced to listen to reality. He tried his old tricks of smiling and threatening. When that did not work, he flew into fits of rage. But the staff did not budge. His manipulations had been revealed for what they were. In the end, he admitted his illness and promised to be better. Unfortunately, my friend says the pastor is still much the same person.

But the difference is in the members of the staff. They had spoken the truth; they were the ones set free. Now, whenever he tries to inflict his illness on them, they immediately expose and reject his manipulation. His power is broken. And though he will not change, they are on the road to health and life.   People often confess that they tell "little, white lies," but they do not "hurt anyone" with them. But, they do hurt someone—themselves.

When we recognize and speak the truth, there is an unshakeable sense of integrity and wholeness. When our interior selves and external actions are harmonious, there is no mask, no deception, no manipulation of others. We radiate simplicity and peace.

We have a choice to make, which our words and actions time and again ratify: we can live a lie or we can choose the truth.

We are afraid of conflict and of being rejected; we hesitate to say anything that might offend someone. If we succumb to the fear, we may find ourselves sacrificing the truth for a moment's ease and a small crack in our inner selves begins. As we travel the road to perdition, the lesion widens and deepens until there is not one but two of us: the false self and the true self. The two are mortal enemies; they are eternally at odds; the battle between them is unending. This inner combat causes a disease, a personality disorder and the pain of the wound begets a rage that will not be quenched. Torn apart by this inner struggle and consumed by rage, we become a clone of the deranged pastor. Then his task is complete—he has made us like himself.

But, if we tell the truth, we have made a choice for freedom. Despite the external conflicts that may arise, inside, there is unity and a true peace. Such holiness and peace give witness to the rightness of our decision and the presence of the Kingdom. Jesus is more than a truth-teller. He is the very incarnation of truth. When we choose the truth, we choose him, for it is Jesus himself who proclaimed, "I am the way, and the truth, and the life" (Jn 14:6).

# 14

# Pray Always

❧  The anonymous author of the spiritual classic, *The Way of a Pilgrim*, began his spiritual journey with a problem. He read in the Scriptures that "it is necessary to pray continuously" (1 Thes 5:17). Though the words "made a deep impression" on him, he did not see how it was possible, due to the "practical necessities of life."[1] He then sought to learn the secret of unceasing prayer.

If "prayer" requires a time set aside to communicate with God, then it is clearly impossible to pray always; there are too many other duties and distractions that require our attention. Only cloistered monks would seem to have the luxury of unceasing prayer.

Some authors would try to resolve this difficulty by taking a more "spiritual" approach to prayer. They propose that true prayer is in the will. Before we begin our day, we should make an act of self-offering to God, they suggest. Thus, the rest of the day will be considered a prayer. While this daily self-offering is to be commended, the idea of a single, brief act resulting in an entire day of prayer is not convincing.

Our spiritual pilgrim had an intuition that prayer is something more than he was taught as a youth. Children learn to pray by *speaking* to God. It is God's duty, then, to listen and respond. Some adults learn more advanced forms of prayer; they learn to *listen* to God. Through reflection on the Scriptures and periods of meditation, God "speaks" to the soul. Thus, they "hear his voice."

But there is one step in prayer that is left. These first two steps, *speaking to God* and *listening to God*, are part of any religion—all spiritual disciplines propose such forms of prayer. Prayer, however, is an outgrowth of theology and, conversely, true theology emerges from prayer. Thus, because of its unique message, Christianity must offer something more, a new possibility in prayer. We are not disappointed.

After a worship service an older woman said that she is constantly aware of God's presence; it is almost palpable. When I asked her what it felt like, she said, "Well, it is hard to describe. I have a great sense of peace. I can feel that God is with me. At times, this presence becomes so strong, I am filled with joy, and people tell me that my face seems to radiate his presence."

"Has it changed your perspective of the world?" I asked her. "Yes," she responded, "it is as if the world has a new dimension to it, a deeper dimension. I did not realize it before, but my vision of the world used to be two dimensional—flat. Now, everything is intense and alive. All creation sparkles with life!"

I have been surprised by the great number of people who have this awareness of God's presence, especially among the elderly. Perhaps it is due to a lifetime of purification and prayer preparing them to receive so great a gift. It is, indeed, a grace. Theologians of the mystical life have called it an infused awareness of God's presence. Many of us still must make acts of faith that God is present; they know it by experience.

Some people believe that faith is a completely blind trust in a remote and hidden God. For other religions this might be true, but it cannot be so for Christianity. We celebrate God's presence in our world, a presence we call the Kingdom. Because of this event, we are surrounded by God; we walk in a sea of God's presence. Truly, "in him we live and move and have our being" (Acts 17:28).

Jesus said it clearly: "The reign of God is already in your midst" (Lk 17:21). It seems strange to us that someone would constantly be aware of this reality, this presence of God. However, I recall an Asian story that seems appropriate: An old master was conversing with a young disciple. The youth was so surprised at the master's depth of awareness. "Old Man, how is it that you see such things?" And the master responded, "Young Man, how is it that you do not." Perhaps the consciousness of the elderly to the Kingdom of God is the rule and not the exception.

Most of us are somewhere on the road to this new horizon of consciousness. If we have not yet attained the spiritual vision of this woman, we do see signs of it occasionally. Sometimes the most ordinary events disclose the deeper reality: the miracle of a newborn, the love of a young man and woman, the peaceful death of a parent. All are possible vehicles for the Kingdom as God's presence shines through every event, every moment, every face.

To know this, to become one with God, to be constantly aware of the Kingdom—this is the secret of unceasing prayer. "It is a great gift," you say, "one far beyond me." Certainly, but Christianity of its very nature is such a gift.

When it is fully realized, we too walk in the Kingdom; we too are constantly aware of God's presence; we too pray unceasingly.[2]

We have a long way to go. Many of us may not even finish. It is no matter. The greatest mystery of Christianity is the mystery of redemption. We do not need to finish the race—few of us do. We need only give God a moment, the barest opening. Then the one who is the very source of time will turn a moment into eternity. In "the twinkling of an eye" (1 Cor 15:52), "all things will be made new" (Rv 21:5).

# Discussion Questions

1. Does the message of the Kingdom make me uncomfortable? If not, why not? If so, what challenges me?

2. Do I sometimes feel "enthused," filled with the Spirit? Where does this "fire" in my heart lead me?

3. What are my sins I am aware of? What keeps me from becoming more aware of my faults and sins? How can these sins be "doors" through which I enter the Kingdom?

4. What are the choices I have made, and will make, that mean spiritual life or death for me? How have my choices transformed me? Do I like the person I am becoming?

5. What are the "crosses" in my life? Are some of them self-inflicted? What are my true crosses and how is God turning them into sources of life for me?

6. Do I speak the truth with courage? Are there situations in which I hesitate to tell the truth, even when I feel called to do so? How might I live a more honest and authentic life?

# WHAT IS
# THE KINGDOM LIKE?

# 15

## An Absurdity to the Gentiles

☙ When we think of power, we think of it in active, aggressive, even dominating terms. The Romans, for example, were powerful. They imposed their will on the world by the force of their legions. They cared little for the feelings of their slaves.

The Jewish people knew that Yahweh, their God, was supremely powerful. He was their champion and they longed for the day when he would come to save them. He would send them an anointed one, a Messiah, who would deliver his people from oppression and the dominating rule of Rome. Finally, the long awaited day did arrive. But instead of entering the Holy City astride a horse and leading a victorious army, as did Roman conquerors, this man rode on an ass, followed by people waving palm branches (Mt 21:7-8).

The difference is startling. Is this the great anointed one of God who will deliver his people? Isaiah's words were ascribed to him: "The bruised reed he will not crush; the smoldering wick he will not quench" (Mt 12:20). It was a display of a type of power that they had never before experienced.

In the East there is a symbol of this sort of power: water. Water flows downhill; it does not insist on having its own way. Soft and malleable, flexible and agreeable, it simply flows where it is led. To witness the efficiency of this sort of power, one need only look at the Grand Canyon, where water cut this wonder out of rock. Such was the power of this anointed one of God.

But, then, another startling revelation about the anointed one came to light. This humble Messiah, this prophet from God, claimed to be God's son. As Scripture says, he "was speaking of God as his own Father, thereby making himself God's equal" (Jn 5:18). Two thousand years ago, the High Priest posed a question to the Sanhedrin concerning this claim. Now, this question is addressed to us: "You have heard the blasphemy. What is your verdict" (Mk 14:64)? To the charge of claiming to be God's equal, the Scriptures themselves testify that Jesus is guilty!

Can the almighty God take a human form? Is it even possible that Yahweh, the source of all, could walk the face of the earth? In all fairness to the High Priest, it is a blasphemous notion. It is hard enough to believe that the omnipotent God would not lead a conquering army to destroy the Roman rule. Now we are asked to believe that the eternal God could enter this world and experience our human existence with all its struggles, toils, heartbreaks, and fears.

If this were not enough, this Messiah of the omnipotent

God then "delivered himself into the hands of men" who killed him (Lk 9:44). The idea of God dying on the cross is ludricrous. Sacred Scripture records that this was "a stumbling block to Jews, and an absurdity to Gentiles" (1Cor1:23). What kind of power is it that not only takes on the form of his own creatures, but then allows himself to be tortured by them, disgraced, and put to death?

Jesus addressed the problem directly: "The Son of Man has not come to be served but to serve—to give his life in ransom for the many" (Mk 10:45). He even tells a parable of what it will be like with his heavenly Father. He, too, in the fullness of his Kingdom, will serve them. "I tell you, he will put on an apron, seat them at table, and proceed to wait on them" (Lk 12:37). Jesus symbolically enacts this truth when, at the Last Supper, he washes their feet.

How strange! The power of God is a humble one, meek and lowly, riding into Jerusalem astride a colt (Mt 21:5). The almighty God comes to serve his own creatures. Little wonder that so many of his contemporaries did not recognize Jesus as the Messiah of God. He was not the image of God they were looking for.

No wonder that they decided to kill him. This humble power was a force eminently more potent than anything they had ever encountered. It threatened every religious notion and challenged their entire horizon of consciousness. They had either to undergo a complete transformation of mind and soul, or destroy the source of the challenge. History records the choice they made.

Jesus invites us to be like him and his heavenly Father. He tells us: "You know how among the Gentiles those who seem to exercise authority lord it over them; their great ones make their importance felt. It cannot be like that with you. Anyone among you who aspires to greatness must serve the rest" (Mk 10:42-43). Thus,the Kingdom of God belongs to the little ones.

Even now this power of God is persuasive and gentle; it does not coerce. It goes into a heart only when invited; it does not force its way in. For example, when people undergo a radical conversion they are initially thrilled to experience the grace of God in their lives. They feel God's love and joy, and find it easy to open the doors of their hearts to this Spirit. But when the "honeymoon" is over and the consolations are less frequent, the real struggles of the Christian life become more palpable. Inevitably a difficult question arises: "Do I want to continue in this rugged spiritual journey?" Some have asked me directly, "Can I quit?" "Yes," I tell them, "you can quit. God will not enter where he is not wanted. The decision is yours." Some do quit. But those who leave the Christian path usually don't ask the question directly; they just quietly fade away and find new interests and excitements.

It should not be surprising that even today many of us do not recognize the anointed one of God in our midst. He is not what we expect because we do not know God or the Kingdom of God.

To serve, to persuade, to love but always allowing the freedom of the loved one to say no, this is the Kingdom of God. It is an unexpected reality: a God who becomes human, a conqueror astride a colt, a Messiah who liberates by dying.

# 16

## My House Shall Be Full

ᑫᕈ   Many years ago a wealthy Jewish man moved to
an island off the North Carolina coast. Two groups of people lived there: well-to-do summer folk who vacationed on
the island, and the "locals" who lived there all year and
barely eked out a living. To introduce himself, the man decided to have a party and invite all the wealthy summer
folk. He hired a band and spared no expense preparing the
lavish event. The invited guests all said they would come
but secretly conspired not to attend. He was the first and
only Jewish person on the island and, in their bigotry, they

rejected him. When it came time for the lavish affair, no one arrived, and the man realized why. So, he turned to the servants who had prepared the feast and to the poor people on the island and urged them to come. They were excited about being invited and came gladly. Everyone had an enjoyable time and decades later the people still recall that wonderful evening with delight.

This true story bears a striking resemblance to the parable that Jesus told about the king giving a wedding banquet for his son. The nobility refused to come so he had his servants go into the highways and invite anyone they could find. He then says an important line: "I want my house to be full" (Lk 14:16-24, Mt 22:2-10). In this parable, Jesus compared the Kingdom of God to a great banquet or a special celebration. God the Father, like any host, wishes it to be a joyous occasion with a house full of guests. But the people who should come, those we would expect to attend, do not.

This was the experience of Jesus. In the name of God the Father, the Son invited the obvious guests, the chosen people of Israel. He likewise appealed to the religious leaders and "holy" people of the day, those who kept the law. They did not respond. Rather, it was the outcasts of Jewish society that followed him—the poor, lame, blind, and lepers.

In his parables, he constantly held up figures outside the "law" as worthy of emulation. He commended a Samaritan and a Roman centurion; he proclaimed to the righteous that "the tax collectors and prostitutes are entering the Kingdom of God before you" (Mt 21:31).

Such actions outraged the leaders. These people were all untouchables; their professions set them outside of God's protection. Jesus not only accepted them, he said they held a favored place in his Father's house.

Astounding! In the Kingdom of God there is a reversal of expected human values and expectations. Nowhere did Jesus say it more clearly than when he declared, "The last shall be first and the first shall be last." The Kingdom is paradoxical—just when you think you understand it, it reverses itself again and you are surprised and dumbfounded.

For example, we expect that someone who sins least will be held in the highest regard. After all, sin is bad and righteous deeds are good. But in a meal with Simon, a Pharisee, Jesus blasts this expectation with a parable about two men who owed a debt. The one who was more grateful, and thus held up as exemplary, was the one whose larger debt was remitted—the greater sinner (Lk 7:43).

St. Paul struggled with this Kingdom reversal when he said, "Where sin abounds, grace abounds all the more." In the Kingdom, sin is like a magnet; mysteriously, it attracts grace, and when the grace is received, the body is much stronger because of the healing of its former infirmity. It is like a bone that is strongest in the place where a former break has knitted.

There was a man named Gene in a parish where I was assigned. Were it not for some assistance from society, he would have lived on the streets. They housed him in a home for the elderly and a kind, religious Sister looked after his needs. He would wear the same smelly clothes until she finally peeled them off him and insisted he put on the clothes she provided him.

Each morning when I unlocked the church, Gene would be sitting in the doorway, where he had been for some time in the cold. He grumbled a lot, talked to himself, and had a severe case of epilepsy since childhood. Gene was given to outbursts of swearing, was odd and cantankerous by anyone's estimation, and was generally a nuisance.

But when you talked to him there was a gentleness about the big man. He loved the church, gave what little money he had, and was anxious to help out, although he was too unreliable and uncoordinated to help with much. He attended daily Mass and I would see him praying for long periods.

When he came to communion, he seemed like a different person. His voice was clearer, his eyes brighter, and I often had the impression that he had come to know the ways of deep prayer, a real contemplative union. The only thing Gene did tell me once, after a severe epileptic attack, was, "I don't know why the good Lord is keeping me in this world. I am ready." Indeed, he was.

Gene seemed to be of little use to society, and even to the church. However, when Jesus delivered his Sermon on the Mount, I think it was Gene that he was talking about. As Jesus looked out, he addressed the poor, weak, the discarded, those who had nothing but faith, those whose only consolation was hope. Jesus said they were important; they were blessed; they would be consoled; they would have their fill of holiness and mercy.

Then he said something about the present. He said that even now, concerning such people, "The reign of God is theirs" (Mt 5:3). This reign of God, which Jesus not only proclaimed but ushered in through his very being, belongs to them. It is not for the sleek or the self-righteous. It is for the lowly and the poor.

The paradoxical Kingdom made no "sense" in Jesus day and we deceive ourselves if we think it does today. There is no reason why Gene should enter the Kingdom before me, a person who has dedicated his life to spreading the gospel. However, I know he will.

Our Father's house will be full. But those we expect to come will not be there. In a surprising reversal that is a hallmark of the Kingdom, sitting around the banquet table will be the outcasts and public sinners of the world. In the Kingdom, these "last" ones will be first.

# 17

## God Will Come for Me

❧ Have you ever seen someone on the street corner with a sign, "Jesus is coming"? Usually the man is unkempt and appears to be a street person who woke up one morning and decided that God was about to enter his miserable world and change things. As members of the well-kept middle class, we dismiss him as "crazy" and move on. But he does embody a fundamental dynamic in Christian humanity. First of all, this man's life is a mess: physically, emotionally, and we presume, spiritually. His clothes are filthy. He lives on the streets. He has no friends or family nearby. He is not a church member. He is in a miserable state and that morning he wakes up and realizes how miserable it is.

Second, he also realizes that he is powerless to get out of the situation. The middle class usually believes that if he really wanted to better himself, he could clean himself up, get a job, and live a productive, well-ordered life. Much of the time, however, it is not possible. Such people are so emotionally marred that they lack the most basic of social and psychological skills that are essential for fitting into the society that we have constructed. They simply cannot do it, no matter how hard they try.

Finally, with the realization that he was in a situation he hated and was powerless to change it, he was faced with that fundamental human choice: despair or faith. This man chose faith. He even went one step beyond this act of faith: he not only accepted the existence of a good God, but also believed that since this God is good and powerful, and since he is in such a dire situation, this God will come to save him.

At the time of John the Baptist, the Jewish people also believed that God would come to save them. He would send a Messiah. He would deliver the people from their bondage, particularly from the Romans who ruled by the force of their legions. Like the man on the street, they were in a miserable situation, they were powerless to change it, and they knew that only God could save them.

In this Christian era, we believe that the Messiah did come and when he returned to the Father, promised to come again at the end of time. Then the Kingdom of God will be established in its fullness. Its fruits will be joy and peace.

The early Christian church originally believed that this second coming would be soon. They fervently recited a prayer that became part of the official prayer of the church, its liturgy. They said, in Aramaic, *Maranatha*, which means, "O Lord, come"[1] (1 Cor 16:22). Two thousand years later Christ has still not come. The first apostles believed they would not see death before their Master returned for them, but generation after generation has come and gone and still the hope of humanity is not fulfilled.

And yet, the cry is still on our lips—*Maranatha*. It is not just the cry of the Jewish people living in slavery, nor of the first apostles waiting for their beloved Lord to return. It is, as symbolized by the street man carrying the placard, the cry of all humanity. We are filled with pain, incompleteness; we believe in an all-powerful, loving God, and then a fervent hope rises in our hearts: he will come to save us!

In modern times, we have come to project a dangerous lie. Somehow we have agreed that it is not good to admit or show to others that we are in pain, that our lives are not smooth, and that we struggle to maintain our existence. This has given rise to the great illusion that many of us subtly labor under. When pain finally does enter our lives, our minds assure us, "I am the only one who suffers; everyone else is fine." We feel like spiritual lepers, outcasts of society.

But everyone else is not fine. It was the teaching of the Book of Genesis that humanity is saddled with a life of pain and toil. God told Eve, "In pain shall you bring forth children" (3:16) and God condemned Adam to labor by "the sweat of your face...thorns and thistles shall it bring forth to you" (3:19, 18). This is the lot of humanity, to toil in sweat and to labor in pain. When we stop denying this, especially to ourselves, we can begin to live truly. Perhaps we can spiritually catch up to the man with the sign. At least he knows what he is made of. We should be envious of him.

There is another stumbling block to the Christian dynamic of feeling pain, trusting in God, and thus believing in his coming to save us. This block, as destructive as the denial of pain, is a false humility that does not believe itself important enough in God's eyes to warrant his coming. "If God does come," we think, "he will pass me by." It is like children picking sides for a game. There are two young people on one side and a crowd of others huddled together. One by one, the two team captains choose the sleek and the strong from the crowd. Finally, there is one person left over. This one is usually a bit too small or unco-ordinated, not as good as the rest. It is a pitiful sight to see that child standing there, unwanted. We know the sorrow and pain he must feel. We are not so different. Hidden in our hearts is the same sentiment. "If God is coming," we think, "he will visit everyone else but me."

Oddly enough, the one left behind is precisely the one God will visit. He leaves the ninety-nine sheep and searches out the one sheep that is lost (Lk 15:4). Or if he has ten silver pieces and loses one, he will search the entire house to find that one silver piece (Lk 15:8). It is true, we may feel like such spiritual lepers that we cannot imagine God being in-terested in us. Paradoxically, it is for us that he is coming. He knows our pain and hears the cry of our humanity. God, who put that prayer on our lips—*Maranatha*, "O Lord, come"—will not pass us by.

There is another paradox. It is in this Aramaic prayer-word itself. As we have seen, it is a petition invoking the Lord to come. But it can also be a statement about some-thing that has already taken place. *Maranatha* can also mean, "Our Lord has come!" In the early church, this dou-ble meaning well described their circumstance. They be-lieved that in Jesus, their Lord had already come. In this first sense, it was an act of faith. At the same time, it was also a prayer of hope for their final deliverance—"O Lord come; come again and bring the fullness of your Kingdom of light, joy, and peace."

This double entendre expresses our human predicament as well. We live in a world of struggle and pain. The "illu-sion of fine," perpetrated by the middle class, shatters quickly in the face of the tragedy of raw humanity. As peo-ple of faith, there arises in our hearts a hope, an expecta-tion that God will come and deliver his people. We pray with the early Christians, "O Lord, come!" At the same time, a seed of the Kingdom is buried in our hearts. Even at this early stage, it begins to radiate a peace that the world knows not. We feel a steadiness in troubled times, a joy from an unseen source. This joy in the midst of sorrow, this peace in the midst of conflict, proclaim the truth of the message of Jesus that the Kingdom has already come.

It is good to join our voices in communion with Christians of all ages. In our joy and peace we profess that our Lord has come. In our pain and incompleteness, we pray, "*Maranatha*, O Lord, come."

Our humanity expresses the profound reality of the Kingdom of God. It is a mirror reflecting the many truths that make up this heavenly reign. The Kingdom is not only present in all of the body of Christ, it is present in each one of us. In fact, it is for us, the lepers, that God will come. May the prayer of the whole church be on our lips:   *Maranatha*!

# 18

## We Hear His Voice

ﾗ Several years ago in the seminary, I was walking with a fellow student discussing the life of Jesus. We were speaking of him as if we were intimates, personally familiar with his innermost thoughts and motivations. Finally, the other student looked at me and said, "Frankly, I never met the man." It was a stunning comment, all the more shocking because it conveyed a truth.

We ministers, priests, sisters, laity—all of us who have dedicated our lives to Christianity—spend our days preaching and teaching about a man who lived 2,000 years ago in a remote part of the world. We were left with no personal records and have only a collected series of stories whose total contents would not fill a small book. Not only is it true that none of us have ever met Jesus, we know precious little about him.

Yet, the phenomenon of Christianity continues to spread. The books spent explaining the fragments passed down about his life fill entire libraries. We act and speak as if this man were known to us personally. We not only speak with confidence, we are downright adamant. Some have even died defending their beliefs about him.

Once, Jesus addressed a crowd, "Let him who has ears to hear me, hear" (Mk 4:9, 23, Lk 8:8). Obviously, everyone present had ears and could hear him speaking, including the scribes and Pharisees. Thus, on this first level of meaning, Jesus calls everyone to hear him because all of us have ears.

The second level, however, is more penetrating. Though everyone could hear his words, not all heard the Word. Though everyone listened to the man Jesus, not all heard the Son of God. In frustration, Jesus cried out, "Do you still not see or comprehend? Are your minds completely blinded? Have you eyes but no sight? Ears but no hearing" (Mk 8:17b-18)?

Humans have a sense of when someone is listening to them or not. Married people often complain that their spouses do not listen to them. They speak and the other hears the sound of the words, but there is no communication. They do not believe that their words are really being received.

Many times the other person cannot hear the message. He or she may not be able to face the conflict or accept an unwelcomed message. Until the message is received into the heart, their relationship will stagnate. An ideal union in marriage is impossible without an intimate communication of hearts.

Many did not hear Jesus at this level. More important, he communicated the life-giving Word of God. Many could not hear this Word, either. It was no secret that he performed amazing signs and miracles, which even his enemies acknowledged. However, his detractors dismissed him by claiming that his power came from a sinister source. "It is by Beelzebul, the prince of devils, that he casts out devils" (Lk 11:15). They could not hear the Truth.

There is an edifying story told of an Asian youth who decided to learn the path to enlightenment. He attached himself to a Zen master who promised to teach him. For an entire year the student waited on the master, living in his house and attending to his every need. However, he received no instruction. Finally, the student complained to the master, "I have been with you for an entire year, responded to your every need, and yet you have not taught me a thing!" The Zen master was astonished and replied, "When you give me tea, I drink it. When you give me rice, I eat it. When you greet me, I return your greeting. When have I ever ceased teaching you?" According to the spirituality of Zen, the student was being given the most profound instruction, but he was too blind and deaf to receive it.

The deepest truths are communicated on a spiritual "frequency." It is like music played on a pitch that human ears cannot hear. To hear this Zen master, or to hear the Word of God, requires a special awareness, an expanded horizon of consciousness.

In the West, we believe that faith not only fosters this heightened consciousness, but also opens the ears to spiritual sound. When the heart is open, we can listen to a new dimension, a special voice. Jesus said, "My sheep hear my voice" (Jn 10:27).

There are barriers to hearing this voice, to a heightened consciousness, to faith. We call it sin. I remember a man named Timothy, who used to feel pretty confident about himself, his "faith," and his view of the world—and he had no qualms about sharing it with others. Whenever he spoke, it sounded more like a divine pronouncement than a human opinion. Needless to say, his friends were irritated and one day one of them finally had the nerve to tell him. Tim rebelled. He refused to hear what his friend said. "I am not judgmental," he yelled in anger. "You will not listen to what is right. God will punish you for it!"

But the seed had been planted. Tim wrestled for weeks with the truth, one minute denying it, the next admitting that there might be something to it. Haggard and worn in appearance, Tim went through a painful period of upheaval and internal struggle.

Finally, he gave up fighting the truth. "I am judgmental," he confessed. "How have my friends put up with me for all these years?" Although Tim still had a long way to go, he became more tolerant of others and more humble in his own estimation. When I asked him how he felt about this change, he said, "I feel better—freer. I no longer carry around the weight of the world, making judgments about what is right and wrong. I see things as they are. There is more peace."

Something else happened to Tim. Sacred Scripture came alive for him. He said, "All these years so many things in the Bible didn't make any sense to me. Now they seem to leap off the page and speak to me." Tim can now hear this consoling voice of the Scriptures; his obstacle is gone.

"I am the Good Shepherd," says the Lord. "My sheep hear my voice. I know them and they follow me. I give them eternal life" (Jn 10:14, 27-28). We do hear his voice, not as distinct words spoken, resonating through the air, but as a communication that transcends all others, transmitted on a special "frequency," received directly into the heart.

Like my friend in the seminary, none of us has ever "met the man." And yet I believe that when the last day comes and the eighth day begins, we will stand before him face to face. We will peer into his eyes and from a deep part of the soul there will be a glimmer of recognition. He will speak and we will remember the voice. He will smile at us, and we will say, "I knew it was you."

# 19

# Sharers of the Divine Nature

🍂 "The worst epitaph for a person's headstone," a friend once told me, "would be: 'He was a nice guy.'" You can imagine the effect of the minister's words during the man's eulogy, "He never hurt anyone. He never did anything wrong. He was a nice guy." One gets the impression of a lukewarm life.

The Book of Revelation captures the problem: "How I wish you were one or the other—hot or cold! But because you are lukewarm, neither hot nor cold, I will spew you out of my mouth" (3:15-16)! This is not a minor point. The presence of the Kingdom of God calls for a personal and total choice. There can be no hedging. As Jesus said, "He who is not with me is against me, and he who does not gather with me scatters" (Mt 13:30).

A friend once told that for years she was plodding along with her life and thought things were fine. "I couldn't understand why all these preachers seemed so upset and pleading with us all the time. Frankly, I thought they were overdoing the whole thing. Jesus, I felt, was simply a nice guy who talked about loving each other." Then one day, during a parish renewal, the Lord touched her life. "I couldn't believe it," she said. "I had been so complacent. It was like I was asleep and the Lord woke me up. I realize now that I have a lot of catching up to do."

The Christian call is not to lukewarmness; it is a call to be a "living flame of love," using a phrase from John of the Cross. One of the strongest images of our call that Jesus gave us is the transfiguration. On Mount Tabor his clothes became dazzling white, his very being shone like the sun (Mk 9:2-3). He was transfigured by the presence of God, which was the Kingdom breaking into the world.

If the very person of this "God-man" is an astounding reality, our call as "sharers of the divine nature"(2 Pt 1:4) is no less a reality. Just as Jesus was Son of God and one with the Godhead, we are, as adopted daughters and sons, participants in this oneness with God. If the Kingdom broke into the world in Jesus as witnessed by the transfiguration, it is now expanding in the world through us. This is why it is so frustrating to hear people say, "I don't do anything wrong. I am a good Christian." If being a Christian means not doing anything wrong, then indeed you are. But if it means sharing the very life of God, radiating his presence in the world, and bringing forth the Kingdom, then you are a mere ghost of your calling.

The gospel of John is steeped in this realization. Time and again, he repeats this idea: just as the Father lives in Jesus, so does he live in us. And, just as the Father and the Son are one, we are one in him (cf. 14:11, 14:20, 23).

The same insight is found in the writings of the apostle Paul. His letters are opaque until one realizes this core truth: Christ lives in him. The phrase, "in Christ," appears in the Pauline corpus 165 times.[1] He was "seized by Christ" and became one with him. Through this union, he was saved.

What a difference between this understanding of Christianity—a dynamic union with God—and a perspective of not doing anything wrong! How did it happen that we came to interpret the Christian call in such lukewarm fashion? The call to share in the divine nature is like the Kingdom of God itself, a truth that shocks every human sensibility.

The great Rhineland mystic, Meister Eckhart, experienced it. In a burst of mystic hyperbole, he is reputed to have said, "I am God." Such statements rightly earned him the skepticism of the Vatican. But Eckhart truly experienced the Kingdom of God, feeling the divine life of God flowing through the very fiber and marrow of his life. He could only describe the experience as being God.

The sacrament of baptism welcomes someone into a particular Christian community. It erases sin. We become witnesses to Christ before the world. But it has another function that, although equally or more important, is also least mentioned and most forgotten. During the rite of baptism, the minister says, "See that the divine life which God gives is kept safe." Divine life is given, a powerful statement! God shares divine life with the baptized person, who nurtures this gift until it blossoms into the transfiguration.

I cherish the memory of an older monk with whom I once had the pleasure of spending several months. Whenever he stepped into my room in the monastery, I was filled with a sense of well-being. The closer he came to me, his face beaming with warmth and love, the more my heart rose with joy. He was very solicitous and seemed to be pleased to provide for my least need. I felt loved, and whenever I looked at him I could not help but return the affection.

One morning, I injured my back and was forced to limp to his room and ask for help. He was not expecting me since this time was reserved for solitude and prayer. Nonetheless, my back would not wait. So, I knocked and at the sound of his voice opened the door. What I saw inside I will never forget. He was radiant. His robes seemed to shine and his face glowed with a light that was not only spiritual but physical. The scene conveyed a love and peace beyond telling. It was, for me, a grace to be present. Perhaps the even greater grace was spending so many days with him. I experienced the warmth of being loved and the joy of his heart.

Each of us is called to experience this powerful Kingdom of God among us. Our call is no less than to be completely transfigured by it. We are to be filled with the presence of God and to become fully one with him. And, it is not something impossible nor beyond us: "For this command which I enjoin on you today is not too mysterious and remote for you....No, it is something very near to you, already in your mouths and in your hearts; you only have to carry it out" (Dt 30:11, 14).

# 20

# We Will Be "Known" by Jesus

❧ I often think of Mary, a woman who dresses plainly and is bent over from her many years. At first, it is difficult to understand why, since she is not very remarkable and she never says anything of note. In every way, she seems rather ordinary. And yet there is something special about her. When I first met Mary, she had few material possessions, but she always seemed to be full of joy. Later, her husband's lingering illness and death swallowed up what little she had. Still, standing next to her, one has the feeling that she is content and lacks nothing. As a matter of fact, she is constantly telling people how blessed she is.

I remember being with her—she was suffering from severe chest pains—as she was being wheeled into surgery for an emergency operation, one that the doctors did not give her much hope of surviving. Yet, she wanted to thank everyone for being so kind to her. She looked at her daughter and told her how much she loved her. She held my hand and told me how good God had been to her all her life. This was all said as she gritted her teeth through the pain. The stunning part was that she meant every word; all she said was from the core of her heart.

Mary's attitude seems impossible. One would be tempted to meet such people with a healthy skepticism. Too many of them turn out to be wearing paper-thin masks put on by would-be saints. Often it is a shield that keeps them from experiencing the fullness of their humanity. If it is kept in place too long, it eventually will disguise an internal rage and, finally, death.

But there are exceptions. All of us know people like Mary. Spending a few moments with them is enough to convince us of their authenticity; in them there is no guile. The power of their witness compels us to ask, "What is the source of such sanctity? How can we be like them?"

Time and again throughout these reflections, it has been pointed out that being a Christian is more than doing nice things, more than being a likeable person, more than even praying to the one God. Too often, Christianity has been reduced to a part-time occupation or a pious hobby. It is not enough. Jesus himself said that a time will come when people will pound on the doors of the Kingdom but will not be allowed in. They will shout, "We ate and drank in your company. You taught in our streets." But Jesus will reply, "I tell you, I do not know you or where you are from"[1] (Lk 13:26-27). And he will not let them in.

A key to understanding what Christianity truly requires is in this response of Jesus. He said he did not know them. In our Western culture, knowledge is a purely intellectual function. If we say we know someone, we mean that we have met and retain some information about this person. This is not what Jesus meant. The Divine Judge is acquainted with all people and has more intellectual awareness of them than they do of themselves. But in the gospels, to know someone implies much more. When Gabriel told the Virgin Mary that she would conceive a child, she responded, "How can this be, since I do not know man" (Lk 1:34)? In this case, knowledge had a sexual connotation. The Virgin Mary had not been physically united with a man, hence she did not know a man. To know someone implies an experiential awareness of the most intimate kind. [2]

Jesus said, "My sheep hear my voice, I know them and they follow me" (Jn 10:27). In John's gospel, to know continues to imply the deepest union, though not sexual. To know Jesus means to love him and to be one with him. Those, like my friend Mary as well as the Virgin, who listen to his voice do so from the deepest center of their hearts, which are united to him.

Each of us longs to be known by someone else. We have a need to reveal ourselves to another and to be truly heard. In the end, we can only be completely heard when we have revealed ourself completely to another and have been fully united with that person. To be "known" means to be heard and to become one.

Marriage is a limited "taste" of this fulfillment meant for us in God. Husband and wife are to spend their days together, reveal themselves in vulnerability and trust to the other so that the two of them might become one flesh. Thus they are to unite physically in the act of sexual intercourse; they are to share their selves emotionally with the other, and they are to become spiritually one in the bond of marriage. Still, this union of body, mind, and spirit is only a pale reflection of the all-encompassing call of Christian communion.

The naked truth of this Christian union is even more personal, more intimate, and more complete than the institution of marriage. We are not only to hear Jesus' words and follow his example, we are to become completely one with him in the very core of our being, a place that only God can touch. Jesus said, "I am in my Father, and you in me, and I in you" (Jn 14:20). And because he, who abides in us, is the bearer of the Kingdom of God, one could say that "the Kingdom of God is within you."[3]

This was the central experience of Paul, who time and again wrote of being "in Christ" (e.g. 2 Cor 5:17), being "one in Christ" (Gal 3:28), being "under compulsion" to preach (1 Cor 9:16). Finally, he proclaimed that "the life I live now is not my own; Christ is living in me" (Gal 2:20). What Paul experienced on the road to Damascus, we are not completely sure. But it was no passing phenomenon; the Christ he saw dwelled inside him and animated his every step.

For those of us who balk at human intimacy, the radical Christian call to divine union can be terrifying. The fear, which is precisely the fear that accompanies death as well, is that we will become lost, swallowed up, and our own identity destroyed. To surrender to the dark specter of death is but one moment in the total act of surrendering to the awesome darkness of God. There are no controls left, no ways to keep ourselves safe. It is a step into the void.

And yet, it is not a completely blind step. There is a voice that beckons us. Jesus, who is the very incarnation of this union of the divine and human, assures us, "Do not let your hearts be troubled. Have faith in God and faith in me" (Jn 14:1). He said that we cannot live apart from this union. "I am the vine, you are the branches" (Jn 15:5). You must take the step, Jesus says, and you must become one with me. If you refuse, there is only death, for one "who does not live in me is like a withered, rejected branch" (Jn 15:6).

Surprisingly, stunningly, what follows from this union is not annihilation but fulfillment. The mystics call it a spiritual marriage. My friend Mary simply radiates its presence. To become one with the One produces an over-flowing abundance—"love following upon love" (Jn 1:16).

Is there anyone who claims to be a model Christian? Our faith demands more than a few minor adjustments to our personalities. St. Paul says, "If anyone is in Christ, [that person] is a new creation" (2 Cor 5:17). Elsewhere we are admonished to "put on that new [person]" (Eph 4:24). We are the "new wineskins" into which "new wine" is being poured (Mk 2:22). We are not the same people we once were. Like Mary, we have become completely new. And there is something in our world that is forging this new creation. There is a fire on the earth. It is hard to perceive, so blind have we become. And yet it is a raging fire sweeping the earth—challenging, changing, transforming the marrow of all creation until it glows with the divine radiance. To be a Christian is to step into the fire.

This is our call; it is our joy; it is our compulsion. We long to become one—it is our innermost desire. We must do it. It is what Christianity demands. A rose is a symbol of the sweetness and beauty of love; a fire bespeaks an uncontrollable power, purification, light. As the mystical poet said, "All shall be well, and all shall be well, and all manner of thing shall be well...the fire and the rose are one."[4]

# 21

## On the Last Day

?æ Again and again, the gospels bring home the central teaching of Jesus: the Kingdom of God is at hand. Because of this tremendous event, human history has entered a new age. Heaven is on earth; the infinite gulf between creature and Creator is bridged, and God is united with his people. Now, we hear his voice and his presence fills the very marrow of our lives.

But if this wonderful Kingdom has come, if we have already been saved in Christ, why is life so hard? Does suffering exist in the Kingdom? Paul expresses our struggles well: "All creation groans and is in agony even until now" ( Rm 8:22).

First of all, suffering still exists because we are not individually ready to experience the complete revelation of God. More progress is needed in the spiritual life before we can fully see and hear this Kingdom of joy and peace. One of the great desert monks, Abbess Syncletica, described the spiritual journey as setting fire to a wet log. At first, there is much smoke, and because of the smoke, tears. But after the purification is over, there is a consuming fire and there wells up in the soul an ineffable joy. Most of us are still in the initial stage of smoke and tears. [1]

Second, and more important, although the Kingdom of God is now among us, it is yet to be revealed in its fullness. As St. Paul tells us, even though we see, we only "see indistinctly as in a mirror"; though we know God, our "knowledge is imperfect now" (1 Cor 13:12). What we enjoy now, according to Paul, is the "first fruits" (Rm 8:23). We await the day when we shall see Jesus face-to-face. Like the early Christians, we await the return of the Kingdom-bearer.

One night I was sitting with a small group of people, among whom were several priests. During the beginning of the conversation there was a sense of peace and happiness, reminiscent of the words of Psalm 133: "Behold, how good it is, and how pleasant, where brethren dwell as one!" Everyone was sharing friendship and their love of the gospel; truly, the Spirit of God was among us.

Then, one priest began to speak, criticizing what he saw as a lack of faith, spiritual formation, and commitment in the church today. "It wasn't like that in my day," he said. "People learned their prayers and practiced their faith." The rest of his speech was a diatribe against people, the church, and the world. By the time he finished, the joy we felt was gone.

The priest, in the name of Christianity, spoke a message of anger, bitterness, and judgmental pride. He disguised his true message from us and from himself by using Christian-sounding words and phrases. But there should be no mistake—it was the message of evil that he proclaimed. As one of my professors said, "It is easier to preach the bad news than it is the Good News."

The message of Jesus, on the other hand, communicates peace and confidence. Not only is the Kingdom here in its "first fruits," it will be consummated in its fullness; nothing can stop it. This is the fundamental message of the Parable of the Sower. It is allegorized to refer to many different types of responses to the Word: those without understanding, those who have no roots, and those who falter under persecution. Its basic, underlying message, though, is one of assurance. The seed of the Kingdom will eventually yield "grain a hundred- or sixty- or thirty-fold" (Mt 13:8). It will find good soil. It will grow. It will produce abundance.[2]

The Kingdom of God is now moving inexorably toward its completion. Many have tried and will try to stop it, but to no avail. The Pharisees demanded that Jesus silence his disciples, but Jesus replied, "If they were to keep silence, I tell you the very stones would cry out" (Lk 19:40). The very matter of creation proclaims the Good News as it presses toward its completion. The only true choice we have is whether we will be caught up in the transformation of all creation or wait outside where "there will be wailing and grinding of teeth" (Lk 13:28).

Evil cannot win. Good cannot lose. "Now will this world's prince be driven out, and I—once I am lifted up from earth—will draw all people to myself" (Jn 12:31b-32). Actually, it was not much of a fight. There is simply no way a creature could supplant its creator; it is not possible for a dark angel to overcome the blinding light of God.

This is the source of our optimism and our hope. We do not become slaves of negativism or despair, even though we may be called to "fill up what is lacking in the sufferings of Christ" (Col 1:24). We await the "last day" with a confidence and peace that casts out all bitterness and fear (Jn 6:40).

But, for the present, we live in that in-between time: the Kingdom is here but not in its fullness. It is a time of contradiction. The Christian not only laughs but weeps, not only radiates joy but exudes suffering, not only finds life but undergoes death.

I remember well the story of a young man, twenty-two years old, who kept vigil by his mother's deathbed. She had been ravaged by a long bout with cancer and was not a pretty sight. As her death was imminent, he spent an entire night in her room, in waiting and prayer. The next morning, the chaplain walked in and sat down beside him. After a brief conversation, the young man said, "You know, Father, I have lived with my mother for many years. Only now have I come to realize how beautiful she is." This experience witnesses the beauty of God's presence in us as well as our terrible decay in death.

Somehow, for the Christian, these opposites co-exist in a harmony that makes each the more fruitful: joy and sorrow, hope and despair, happiness and pain, life and death. With each passing day we become stronger, our eyes open a bit wider and our ears more attuned to spiritual sounds. We become real and solid, and our consciousness is increasingly aware of a growing presence of God.

All things are working together to bring about the completion of the divine harmony. It will come.

# Discussion Questions

1. Have I ever been surprised by the way God manifested himself to me? What was surprising about it? What did this experience teach me about God and the Kingdom?

2. When am I most like our humble God? Can I recall a situation in which I felt "poor in Spirit?" How can I change my life to be more open to imitating our humble God?

3. What are the situations in my life I have no control over? If I were to open myself up to God in these situations, what might happen?

4. Do I know Jesus? Do I "hear" his voice? Does he hear the voice of my heart as well?

5. Is the Kingdom of God within me? Have I opened my heart completely so that I am known and heard by God? What are the blocks to a full communion between God and me?

6. Do I believe that God cares about me, personally? What are my real doubts and fears about this? Do I look forward to God's coming to save me?

# Conclusion

The message of Christianity is truly radical, incomprehensible, and "blasphemous." Predictably, the reaction of the people to the bearer of this message was extreme. Some loved Jesus intensely. They gave up their former lives to follow him. Eventually, they would come to worship him as well. Others were threatened by him, provoked to anger; they were convinced he was in league with the devil. Eventually, they would be moved to murder.

My fear today is not that we will be moved to anger, but rather that we will not be moved at all. "But because you are lukewarm, neither hot nor cold, I will spew you out of my mouth" (Rv 3:16).

To be spiritually dead is probably not the unending experience of agony and sorrow, nor even the torments of a perpetual rage and despair. Rather, to be dead to God is to be completely blind and deaf—to feel nothing, to hear nothing, to be locked in a cold and lifeless existence.

Gone is our humanity; gone, too, is our share "in the divine nature." Gone are the joys and sorrows, hopes, and fears. We stop hearing and seeing. What is left is a flatness, a two-dimensional living, a polite smile, and a limp handshake.

We have lost much of the context of the words of Jesus. It is hard for us to understand why the people were so challenged and even outraged, why his words were so offensive. We live under a dangerous illusion. We think, "If Jesus were to come again, this time it would be different." But perhaps the reception would be much worse. Jesus might simply be ignored.

Are there fewer sins today? Fewer acts of violence? More understanding between people? A greater respect for the sanctity of life? More peace in the home? Mutual love and respect? It is unlikely.

Professional counselors' and clergy's offices are continually flooded with abused children, emotionally battered spouses, young women who have been treated as sexual objects. Is there more peace in the world? The twentieth century has been a time unparalleled in history for atrocities and war.

Is our religion so different from that of the scribes and Pharisees? Many of our religious leaders are more humble and kind, servants who do not lord it over others. We rejoice in them, but there are many others.

Human sin remains. Two thousand years later it wears different masks, but it is still here. Thus, we continue to fashion a hell for ourselves, and sin continues to blind us to the truth, to the Kingdom of God.

Jesus' stories and his actions were like electric shocks delivered to the soul, jerking us out of our "habitual half-tied vision of things." He was not so much trying to persuade us with intellectual reasoning as he was reaching into our souls and yanking us inside out. To feel that his message is clear and understandable and much in line with our vision of things is to miss it completely.

At least the scribes and the Pharisees recognized the challenge that Jesus offered. There was some hope for them. Jesus recognized this and screamed his words at them. Like a voice trying to pierce layers of deceit, he sought to kindle a hidden spark that was slowly fading. Is there a spark left in us?

There is a fire on the earth, a consuming fire that engulfs and transforms everything in its path. In its wake, some will take on the face of an angel. Others, sadly, will see in the mirror the face of a devil.

Move quickly; the last day approaches. "I tell you, time is short...for the world as we know it is passing away" (1 Cor 7:29, 31). If the Spirit of God moves you, respond now. There may not be a second moment, another chance. I bury too many people who "never got around to it."

"The light is among you only a little longer. Walk while you still have it or darkness will come over you. The one who walks in the dark does not know where he is going. While you have the light, keep faith in the light; thus you will become children of the light. After this utterance, Jesus left them" (Jn 12:35-36).

# Suggested Reading

Hünermann, Peter. "Reign of God." *In Encyclopedia of Theology: The Concise Sacramentum Mundi*, pp. 1349-1357. Edited by Karl Rahner. New York: Seabury, 1975.

Jeremias, Joachim. *Rediscovering the Parables*. New York: Charles Scribner's Sons, 1966.

Senior, Donald, CP. "Reign of God." In *The New Dictionary of Theology*, pp. 851-861. Edited by Joseph A. Komonchak, *et al*. Wilmington, Del.: Michael Glazier, 1987.

Willis, Wendell, ed. *The Kingdom of God in 20th-Century Interpretation*. Peabody, Mass.: Hendrickson, 1987.

# Scriptural Index to Kingdom (or Reign) of God Citations With Lectionary Cross-References

Each of the following biblical citations mentions the Kingdom, or Reign, of God. The numbers following these citations refer to sections, not pages, and indicate where these citations may be found in the lectionary. The numbers without parentheses refer to Scripture readings taken from the lectionary for Sunday and weekday liturgies. The numbers inside parentheses refer to readings from the proper of saints, commons, ritual Masses, and other special Masses.

**Matthew**

| | | | |
|------|-----------------------------|-------|----------------------|
| 3:2  | 4                           | 13:19 | 399                  |
| 4:17 | 68, 213                     | 13:24 | 107, 400             |
| 4:23 | 68                          | 13:31 | 410                  |
| 5:3  | 71, 359, (667, 742, 767,    | 13:33 | 401                  |
|      | 778, 825, 835)              | 13:38 | 402                  |
| 5:10 | 71, 359, (667, 742, 767,    | 13:41 | 402                  |
|      | 778, 825, 835)              | 13:43 | 402                  |
| 5:19 | 77, 240                     | 13:44 | 110, 403, (742)      |
| 5:20 | 77                          | 13:45 | 110, 403, (742)      |
| 6:10 | 226, 368, (749)             | 13:47 | 110, 404             |
| 7:21 | (778)                       | 13:52 | 110, 404             |
| 8:11 | 176, 376                    | 16:19 | 122, 410, (535 591,  |
| 8:12 | 376                         |       | 724)                 |
| 9:35 | 181, 384, (612, 773, 810)   | 18:1  | 414, (649, 650, 742) |
| 10:7 | 385, 386, (580)             | 18:3  | 414, (649, 650, 742) |
| 11:11| 7, 185                      | 18:4  | 414, (649, 650, 742) |
| 11:12| 185                         | 18:23 | 131, 239, 416        |
| 12:28| —                           | 19:12 | 417, (736, 742, 788) |
| 13:11| 104, 398                    | 19:14 | 418                  |

**Matthew**

| | | | |
|---|---|---|---|
| 19:23 | 420, (513, 788) | 23:13 | 425 |
| 19:24 | 420, (513, 788) | 24:14 | — |
| 20:1 | 134, 421 | 25:1 | 155, 429, (736, 742, 788, 793) |
| 20:21 | 233, (605) | | |
| 21:31 | 137, 189 | 25:34 | 161, 225, (539, 673, 742, 793, 865) |
| 21:43 | 140, 235 | | |
| 22:2 | 143, 422 | 26:29 - | |

---

**Mark**

| | | | |
|---|---|---|---|
| 1:15 | 23, 69, 305, (724, 890) | 10:23 | 144, 347, (742, 810) |
| 3:24 | 90, 317 | 10:24 | 144, 347, (742, 788, 810) |
| 4:11 | 319 | | |
| 4:26 | 93, 321, (855) | 10:25 | 144, 347, (742, 788, 810) |
| 4:30 | 93, 321 | | |
| 9:1 | — | 12:34 | 153, 242, 356, (761) |
| 9:47 | 138, 344 | 14:25 | 169, (909, 921) |
| 10:14 | 141, 346, (742, 756, 761) | 15:43 | (799) |
| 10:15 | 141, 346, (742, 756, 761) | | |

---

**Luke**

| | | | |
|---|---|---|---|
| 1:33 | 11, 197, (545, 653, 689, 712) | 9:62 | 100, 457, (742 788, 810) |
| 4:43 | 433 | 10:9 | 103, 458, (661, 724, 773) |
| 6:20 | 79, 439 | | |
| 7:28 | 191 | 10:11 | 103, 458 |
| 8:1 | 447 | 11:2 | 112, 463, (749) |
| 8:10 | 448, (767) | 11:20 | 241, 465 |
| 9:2 | 451 | 12:32 | 118, (742) |
| 9:11 | 170, (909) | 13:18 | 480 |
| 9:27 | — | 13:20 | 480 |
| 9:60 | 100, 457, (742, 788, 810) | 13:28 | 124, 481 |
| | | 13:29 | 124, 481 |

**Galatians**
    5:21    469

**Ephesians**
    5:5    —

**Colossians**
    1:13    434
    4:11    —

**2 Thessalonians**
    1:5    425

**2 Timothy**
    4:18    151, (591)

**Hebrews**
    1:8    —
    12:28    —

**James**
    2:5    129, 338
    2:8    338

**2 Peter**
    1:11    —

**Revelations**
    1:9    46
    5:10    500, (898, 911)
    11:15    —
    11:17    —
    12:10    (647, 714)

# Notes

## Introduction

1. For a list of these references to the Kingdom (or Reign) of God, see the Scriptural Index at the end of this book.

## Chapter 2

1. Francois Jamart, *Complete Spiritual Doctrine of St. Therese of Lisieux*, trans. Walter Van DePutte (New York: Alba House, 1961) p. 168.

2. Anna Maria Reynolds, C.P., "Woman of Hope," in *Julian: Woman of Our Day*, ed. Robert Llewelyn (Mystic, Conn.: Twenty-Third Publications, 1987) p. 12.

## Chapter 5

1. *The Liturgy of the Hours*, Vol. IV (New York: Catholic Book Pub. Co., 1975), p. 1997.

## Chapter 6

1. John L. McKenzie, S.J., *Dictionary of the Bible* (New York: Macmillan Pub. Co., 1965), p. 765.

2. Ibid., p. 707.

3. Thomas Merton, *The Asian Journal* (New York: New Directions, 1973), pp. 233-236.

## Chapter 10

1. Joseph A. Fitzmyer, *The Gospel According to Luke, X-XXIV*, in The Anchor Bible, Vol. 28A (Garden City, N.Y.: Doubleday & Company, 1985), pp. 1220-1222, 1225.

## Chapter 11

1. St. John of the Cross, *The Collected Works of St. John of the Cross*, translated by Kieran Kavanaugh and Otilio Rodriguez (Washington, D.C.: Institute for Carmelite Studies, 1979), p.312.

## Chapter 14

1. Helen Bacovcin, trans., *The Way of a Pilgrim* (Garden City, N.Y.: Image Books, 1978), p. 13.

2. For further discussion see Brother Lawrence of the Resurrection, *The Practice of the Presence of God*, translated by John J. Delaney (Garden City, N.Y.: Image Books, 1977), p.112.

## Chapter 17

1. John L. McKenzie, S.J., *Dictionary of the Bible* (New York: Macmillan Publishing Co., 1965), p. 541.

## Chapter 19

1. Joseph A. Fitzmyer, "Pauline Theology," in *Jerome Biblical Commentary*, ed. by Raymond E. Brown et al. (Englewood Cliffs, N.J.: Prentice-Hall, Inc., 1968), p. 823.

## Chapter 20

1. This translation of Lk 13:27 is found in Joseph A. Fitzmyer, *The Gospel According to Luke, X-XXIV*, in The Anchor Bible, Vol. 28A (Garden City, N.J.: Doubleday, 1985), p. 1020.

2. John L. McKenzie, S.J., *Dictionary of the Bible* (New York: Macmillan, 1965), pp. 485, 487.

3. For a discussion of this translation of Lk 17:21 see: Joseph A. Fitzmyer, *The Gospel According to Luke, X-XXIV*, p. 1161.

4. T.S. Eliot, *Four Quartets* (New York: Harcourt Brace Jovanovich, 1971), p. 59.

## Chapter 21

1. Helen Waddell, *The Desert Fathers* (Ann Arbor, Michigan: University of Michigan Press, 1957), p. 68.

2. Joachim Jeremias, *Rediscovering the Parables* (New York: Charles Scribner's Sons, 1966), p. 120.